Mr. + Mrs. L

JOY WAY

JOY WAY

*An Expositional Application of the Epistle
to the Philippians*

by

GUY H. KING

MARSHALL, MORGAN & SCOTT LTD.
LONDON :: EDINBURGH

MARSHALL, MORGAN AND SCOTT, LTD.
33 LUDGATE HILL, LONDON, E.C.4

U.S.A.

VAN KAMPEN PRESS
222 EAST WILLOW STREET
WHEATON, ILLINOIS

CANADA

EVANGELICAL PUBLISHERS
366 BAY STREET
TORONTO

First published 1952
Second Impression 1954

MADE AND PRINTED IN GREAT BRITAIN BY
MORRISON AND GIBB LIMITED, LONDON AND EDINBURGH

DEDICATION

TO

THOSE GREAT VETERANS OF FAITH,
AND OF THE GOSPEL

THE REV. J. RUSSELL HOWDEN, B.D.

AND

THE REV. W. W. MARTIN, M.A.

———

*Who have greatly honoured me with their affection,
and inspired me with their example*

FOREWORD

THE roads in Beckenham are so often called Ways—there is Abbots Way, Beck Way, Manor Way, Lloyd's Way, Whitecroft Way, Druid's Way, Goodhart Way, Hayes Way, Malmain's Way, Overhill Way, Wickham Way, Altyre Way, Aviemore Way, Bolderwood Way, Bramley Way, Bushey Way, Village Way— and a score of others.

But there is no Joy Way, so I thought I would remedy the omission. For as we make our journey through this Epistle to the Philippians, taking in the attractive features and views of the roadway, noticing especially the Wonderful Residence " in " which the Christians live, and marking the almost unclouded sunshine throughout its length, we feel that " Joy Way " is the very name for this heavenly street. Come with me then, and let us enjoy a walk together.

G. H. K.

CHRIST CHURCH VICARAGE,
BECKENHAM

CONTENTS

SALUT D'AMOUR

PHILIPPIANS i. 1–2

THE opening of this Epistle is different from that of most in one very interesting particular. It is a difference shared by all three of the Macedonian Epistles—this, and the two to the Thessalonians —and by the little personal note to Philemon. It consists in the somewhat noteworthy absence of the word " apostle ". In all his other letters, Paul feels it incumbent upon him to remind his readers that he writes with all the weight that his sublime position gives him ; he will have occasion to administer rebuke, and, sometimes, rather bluntly, to give directions—and lest, because he was their friend, they might treat his words not too seriously, he takes care to let them understand that he speaks with authority, and that they must give due and proper heed to what he says. But his case is otherwise when he writes to his beloved Philippians. " The church at Philippi ", says Dr. Graham Scroggie, " was almost quite free from those errors which beset so many of the churches of that day " ; and he goes on to quote Professor Findlay as saying, " This is an epistle of the heart, a true love letter, full of friendship, gratitude, and confidence ". There is, we feel, no need to obtrude his apostleship here ; and so his opening greetings are not inappropriately described as a " salut d'amour "—his letter will be found to be full of Joy, and his heart to be full of Love. As we turn, then, to examine the inspired sentences which introduce this moving document, we are likely to be arrested at the outset by—

THE DESCRIPTION OF THE CHRISTIANS

It is given in terms of their relationship to the Lord JESUS CHRIST : and that must, of course, ever be remembered to be the true starting-point of all Christian experience, and all Christian instruction. We do well, in taking up the study of any of the Epistles, to enquire carefully into that matter of where we stand in reference to Him. The Epistles are, in a fundamental sense, the property of believers—they have, except incidentally, nothing to say to the people of the world—their message is addressed to the Church, the members of His body—their teaching is to be grasped and enjoyed only by those who have been truly " born again " of the same SPIRIT who inspired the writing of the Epistles. We are, therefore, not wasting time if we pause to ask ourselves about our relationship to CHRIST—have we, indeed, received Him into our hearts and lives, as our own personal Saviour ? Only so, have we legitimate entrance to this Treasure House ; if so, we have undisputed access to all its Treasure Trove. Our relationship to Him, then, determines both how we get into it, and what we get out of it. Note what is said here concerning that relationship, for the terms employed are applicable to all believers—both to Paul and Timothy who send forth the Epistle, and to the original, and all subsequent, readers of it : you and me amongst them.

" *The Servants.*" Let it be said at once that the word is far too weak a one to represent the Greek : most of the translators have " bond-slaves "—a conception which would be vividly familiar to every reader of this Letter. Quite a number of them were, or had been, slaves themselves—and the word would catch their attention at once. I say " had been " of some, because the law of manumission would have operated in their case—a price would have been paid, and the slave set free. In his fascinating *Light from the Ancient East,* Dr. Deissmann, pp. 319 ff., has some most interesting paragraphs on this releasing of slaves ; and, with his quick and ready mind, the late Archbishop Harrington Lees, in his *Christ and His Slaves,* made use of the learned Doctor's discoveries to point many a moral concerning spiritual servitude and release. Paul's writings abound in allusions to this last phenomenon. The material and the spiritual are found together in such a passage as I Corinthians vii. 22, " He that is called in the LORD, being a [slave], is the LORD'S freedman : likewise also he that is called, being free, is CHRIST'S [slave] ". When a man becomes a Christian, though materially bound as a slave, he is spiritually freed from bondage to Satan and sin ; on the other hand, such a man, though materially set at liberty, is, in the spiritual sense, bound hand and foot to CHRIST. How Paul himself rejoiced—and even gloried—in this New Slavery. In his letters he so constantly uses the word as indicating his relationship to JESUS CHRIST. He would so readily enter into the attitude of the well-satisfied slave of Exodus xxi. 5, " I love my Master. . . . I will not go out free ". From the bondage of sin, the believer has, by the manumission price of " the precious Blood ", I Peter i. 18–19, been set free—only to find himself thereby committed to a bondage more binding than ever. Yet, this time the "service is perfect freedom", the bonds are honourable and sweet. And, for our encouragement, let us remember that (i) *The Master is responsible for His slaves' needs*—feeding, housing, clothing, and all else is the slave-owner's concern. It is because we are GOD'S servants (slaves) that our LORD says "*Therefore* . . . take no thought . . .", Matthew vi. 24–5, for the ordinary needs of life. Our apostle will say later in this very Epistle, iv. 19, "My GOD shall supply all your need". Also (ii) *The Master is responsible for His slaves' duties*—they will not choose their own task, or their own sphere. Whether ours is to be the more menial, or the more genial, work is in His plan, not ours. It is the Christian's wisdom to stand before Him as those in II Samuel xv. 15, "Thy servants are ready to do whatsoever my Lord the King shall appoint", or as Gabriel in Luke i. 19, "I . . . stand . . . and am sent. . . .". Then, too (iii) *The Master is responsible for his slaves' supplies*— "Who goeth a warfare any time at his own charges ? " asks I Corinthians ix. 7 : the soldier has all his military equipment provided ; and likewise, the slave is supplied with everything needful for the adequate discharge of all his duties. Whatever He tells us to do, we can do—" If . . . GOD command thee . . . thou shalt be able to. . . ." Exodus xviii. 23—because all supplies are at our disposal. And as Paul records, in II Corinthians xii. 9, " My grace is sufficient for thee ".

" *The Saints.*" All GOD'S people are thus designated—the sense of the word being " set apart ", or " consecrated " ; and this quite irrespective of personal character. As Lightfoot points out, " Even the irregularities and profligacies of the Corinthian Church do not forfeit it this title ". Yet, be it said that those who are *positionally* holy are expected to be *practically* holy. I am always intrigued by the way it is put in Romans i. 7, and in I Corinthians i. 2, " called to be saints "—where the " to be " is printed in italics, as indicating that those words are not in the Greek but are introduced by the translators to give what they deem to be the sense. But just " called saints " would be accurate, wouldn't it ? In this very Epistle they are " called saints ", and in others ; it is one of GOD'S names for His own. Yes, but as soon as we are " called saints " we are " called *to be* saints " ! To be what we are. There would be something wrong about a prince living like a pauper, about an Englishman masquerading as an alien, about a grown-up person behaving like a child—no, let's be what we are. If, by GOD'S mercy and grace, we are Christians, let us in all things comport ourselves as such ; if we

are " called saints ", we are most assuredly " called to be saints " :
let our conduct, then, be " as becometh saints ", Ephesians v. 3,
in all respects. What a tremendous impression would be made
upon the world if only we Christians were what we are. It is
one of the world's most damaging accusations against us that
we do not act up to our profession. A Christian is a " Christ's
one " : let him, then, be Christly—to use the word that W. Y.
Fullerton was so fond of. Come now, how much of this true
saintliness is there about us ? Never mind about considering,
or criticising, others—what about ourselves, you and me : do
Name and Nature coincide ? Whether we be " bishops "
(" presbyters ", Lightfoot), or " deacons ", or members of the
rank and file, we are all to be saints. Here, then, in these two
great words, " servants " and " saints ", we have the apostle's
description of Christians everywhere. Let us pass on to observe—

The Dwelling-place of the Christians

The particular believers addressed in this letter are said to
live (i) *At Philippi*. It was an interesting city. (*a*) *Geographically*
—it was situate on the great high road between Europe and
Asia, and so possessed great strategic importance. Let it be
noted that Paul, with astute generalship, always, for the spread
of the Gospel, had his eye upon the big centres of population,
trade, learning, or government. Hence his purposeful longing
" I must . . . see Rome ", Acts xix. 21, and his " good cheer "
in the assurance, " thou must bear witness at Rome ", Acts
xxiii. 11. (*b*) *Naturally*—its surrounding land was favoured with
a particularly fertile soil, and nearby were gold and silver mines.
In Paul's eye, just the spot for the sowing of the Gospel seed of
the Word, and the mining of precious souls for the Kingdom. (*c*) *Historically*—it ran back to the ancient times of the
Phœnicians. Subsequently, Philip of Macedon re-established
it, giving it his own name. In its neighbourhood, in 42 B.C.,
Octavian defeated the republican forces, and in honour of his
victory made it a Roman " colony ". Acts xvi. has a number of
allusions which reflect the pride of the inhabitants in their
Roman citizenship, a privilege which, as we know, Paul also
enjoyed and prized. Lightfoot has this delightful note respecting
our present Epistle, " Addressing a Roman colony from the
Roman metropolis, writing as a citizen to citizens, he recurs to
the political franchise as an apt symbol of the higher privileges
of their heavenly calling, to the political life as a suggestive
metaphor for the duties of their Christian profession '.

(d) *Biblically*—it is the place where the Gospel was first preached in Europe. Paul, seemingly to his surprise (for he had quite different plans, Acts xvi. 6–7) found himself at Troas, where he had his vision calling him to Macedonia. And now he knew why his own programme had been summarily brushed aside, for he was actually at the seaport whence he could travel direct to Europe. Imagine his excited zeal when he set forth. Even the elements seemed to speed him on his journey [as " the stars in their courses " helped forward another project, Judges v. 20] for his boat accomplished in two days, Acts xvi. 11, a journey which, in other conditions, took five days, Acts xx. 6. What a great sequence of conquests we find in this city—amongst them, those two converts : the one, that of the capable business woman, so quiet—Lydia's heart was opened ; the other, that of the gaoler, so catastrophic—his whole being was shaken. Thus Paul was used to the winning of these two hearts, and became ever welcome to their two houses. They were the first-fruits of the Gospel, the nucleus of the Church that grew up around them : a Church that never forgot what they owed to the apostle, a Church that begat in him an undying affection, as this Epistle he wrote them abundantly reveals. If we may, as many think, include that soothsaying damsel as also a convert, we have here, as Lightfoot points out, the gaining for CHRIST of a Jewish proselytess, a Greek slave, and a Roman gaoler—female, as well as male ; bond, as well as free; Gentile, as well as Jew, as Galatians iii. 28 would lead us to expect. Or, as it thrilled me to recall—" Hebrew and Greek and Latin," as His kingly title, in John xix. 20, prophesied.

But while these believers were resident in Philippi, let it be noted that they enjoyed a more intimate environment and dwelling-place (ii) " *In* CHRIST ". Herein lay (a) *Their protection from evil life.* The moral condition of a heathen city would be a constant peril to any new converts, especially as they themselves had but just recently come out of that very heathenism. Philippi may not have been so utterly debased as Corinth, or Rome, but its atmosphere must have been a subversive influence threatening any who would live pure and true. Yet, they could be kept safe. Christians must, of course, remain in such hostile surroundings, for CHRIST must have there, as Matthew v. 13–14 teaches, the salt, the light, and the testimony. So He Himself prays " not that Thou shouldst take them out of the world, but that Thou shouldst keep them from the evil ", John xvii. 15. That keeping, that protection, is ministered to us in the fact of our being, not only " in the world ", but more closely, " in

CHRIST ". A shipwrecked man writes a message, and throws it
into the sea, in the hope that it may reach some shore. But
will not the water damage and destroy it ? No ; for, while it
is cast into the sea, it is first sealed in a bottle—and so it arrives.
Yes ; in Philippi, with all its destructive influences, but " in
CHRIST "—so they are secure, and so, in spite of all antagonistic
forces, they arrive at " the haven where they would be ". Herein
lay also (b) *Their possibility of holy life.* We are called not only
to a negative but to a positive life—" eschew evil, and do good ",
as I Peter iii. 11 says. But how can a holy life be lived in such
unholy surroundings ? Mark that little water-spider going down
to the bottom of that pond. It doesn't really belong there, even
as we believers are " in the world . . . [but] not of " it, John
xvii. 11, 16. The little creature has the queer, and amazing,
ability of weaving a bubble of air around itself, and hidden in
that it is able to pursue its way even amid such inimical conditions—in the water, but in the bubble ! So we come back to our
glorious truth—in Philippi, but " in CHRIST " ; then even in the
midst of the most uncongenial surroundings, the CHRIST-life
can be lived. As we study this Epistle, reading between the lines,
we shall see how splendidly these first European believers
learned the lesson, and practised the art. We, too, in our dual
dwelling, shall find all our needed protection, and realise all our
great possibility. And now let us turn to a third main thought
of this introductory section—

THE DESIRES FOR THE CHRISTIANS

" Grace and peace "—just the customary greeting : " grace ",
the Western, " peace ", the Eastern ; but when the HOLY SPIRIT
led Paul to combine them here, we may be sure that He intended
their use to be something so much more than formal and usual ;
both writer and readers would be led to see in them very deep
and rich meaning. Bishop Wilson Cash makes the interesting
suggestion that " St. Paul combines both Jewish ' peace '
and Gentile ' grace ' in one salutation as a pledge of unity
between East and West, between Jew and Gentile, in the one
Saviour, who unites all in the one fellowship of His Body ".
Dr. Hugh Michael, in the Moffatt Commentary, speaks of " the
enrichment of the commonplace by the new faith of CHRIST,
which elevates a salutation into a benediction ". How arrest-
ingly that is seen in the transmutation of everything, however
lowly, that He touched—a common Name, a despised City, a
humble Workshop, even a felon's Cross. Dr. Johnson said of

Oliver Goldsmith, " He touched nothing that he did not adorn ' :
how infinitely truer of the Master. So here the common greeting
is invested with uncommon beauty.

What are these things that the apostle desires for his friends,
and which are no less desirable for ourselves ? (a) " Grace "—
a quality which is, at once (i) an Attitude, which He adopts
towards us, as in Ephesians ii. 8 ; (ii) an Activity, which He
exerts for our help, as in I Corinthians xv. 10 ; and (iii) an Accom-
plishment, which He works in, and out from, us, as in Acts iv. 33.
Paul ardently, and prayerfully, desires for his converts everywhere—for he uses the words in all his church letters—that
they may experience to the full this " grace ", which the late
Bishop Handley Maule describes as " love in action ".   Then
comes (b) " Peace "—the " GOD of grace " is the " GOD of
peace ", I Peter v. 10 ; Romans xv. 33 ; and it is only by, and
after, His grace that we can enjoy His peace. Peace of heart
—no condemnation before GOD ; peace of conscience—no controversy with GOD ; peace of mind—no anxiety about life ;
peace of action—no grit in the machinery. This gift is an im-
mensely precious boon ; and it may be the possession, should
be the possession, of every believer. Paul will have some deep
things to say about this later.

These two joys come, says our passage, " from GOD our Father
and the Lord JESUS CHRIST "—the Father is the Source, from
whom they come ; the Saviour is the Medium, through whom
they come. Not from the world arise such blessings, nor from
our circumstances, however affluent and pleasant, nor from our
own inner being, however much we strive, but only from Him,
through Him, and " all the fulness of the godhead . . . and ye
are complete in Him ", Colossians ii. 9–10.

So runs the Love Greeting with which this glorious Letter
opens—Salut d'amour.

THE GOOD COMPANIONS

PHILIPPIANS i. 3–8

IN verse 5 Paul uses the words " your fellowship ", which give the keynote of this section ; and, indeed, the thought is not far away all through the Epistle. Some of the commentators, in fact, consider that " fellowship " is the real theme of the Letter, and there is much to be said for that view.

Here they are, then, the Philippian Christians and the Apostle, the good companions along the way. There are difficulties, of course, and there will be disappointments, perhaps, but judging from what he says, and from what they do, it is a very happy comradeship that they have—for them, at least, it is the Joy Way through life. Mark, please, that it is—

A FELLOWSHIP BEGOTTEN IN LOVE

" Blest be the tie that binds our hearts in Christian love ", sings John Fawcett ; and that should ever be the golden thread uniting all believers. It was one of the characteristics of the early church which so profoundly impressed the pagan onlookers, " See how these Christians love one other ". The very same words are sometimes used by the world concerning us Christians to-day —only now they are spoken ironically ! If only they were employed again as expressive of a reality, how greatly enhanced would be the power of our impact upon our age. Love is still the most impelling force in the universe. I always enjoy that legendary conversation between the Wind and the Sun, arguing which of them was the more powerful. Espying a man on earth heavily overcoated, they conceived the idea of testing their respective power by seeing which of them could the more quickly make him remove his coat. The wind began the contest, blowing his ferocious and icy blasts, only to cause the man to hug himself the tighter in his warm wrappings. Then the sun started, pouring down its rays of heat, with the result that soon first the gloves, then the scarf, came off—and then the overcoat. The sun always wins.

Oh, for a great outpouring of love from the Church upon this poor, chilly world. It must, I think, begin with ourselves—the all-too-frequent criticism, and back-biting, and ignoring of one another must go, and the all-too-rare quality of brotherly concern and loving-kindness must flourish amongst fellow-believers, Galatians vi. 10. We must learn to walk as Good Companions, after the secret of Romans v. 5, " The love of GOD is shed abroad in our hearts by the HOLY GHOST who is given unto us ".

See this true warm affection in our passage. (a) " I have you in my heart " (7). This is better than having people (i) On our minds—for our thoughts about them might be either full of assurance, or full of anxiety, might be glad or sad. In the Philippians' case, Paul says, " it is meet for me to think " well of you ; but it would not be so in every instance. Again, this is better than merely having people (ii) On our lips—to be constantly talking about them, whether for praise or blame. Paul never tired of talking about his beloved converts ; but, then, he did not stop at talking of them to others, but talked about them to GOD. Then, this is better than having people (iii) On our nerves —though we are bound to confess that some folk are uncommonly trying : be it whispered that some of us Christians are amongst the most trying of all—such bores, or such rasps, as we often are. If ever people like—well, if ever people got on Paul's nerves, I am sure that he very soon got rid of them there ; for it was his habit, as it should be ours, to have people (iv) On our hearts— then will their weaknesses and shortcomings be allowed for ; then will their daily needs be catered for, then will their constant welfare be sought for ; then will their deepest blessings be prayed for. There are some ministrations that are not possible to everybody ; but the ministry of kindness, so fruitful for the harvest of the Kingdom, is open to all.

Notice also this further phrase, (b) " How greatly I long after you all " (8). He longs to see them again, as he probably did, after his acquittal and release from his present imprisonment ; for it seems likely that he resumed his journeys for a while in between his two trials, including a proposed visit to Philippi, " I trust in the LORD that I also myself shall come shortly " (ii. 24). He longs to hear how they are faring—" that I may be of good comfort when I know your state " (ii. 19). He longs to thank them personally for all the love gifts of creature comforts that they had sent him—through such as Epaphroditus, " your messenger ". (ii. 25). He longs that, in their turn, they may have the very deepest, highest, widest, richest blessings that GOD can impart, and so for " this I pray " (i. 9). All these longings are quickened by, measured by, and constrained by, " the yearnings of JESUS CHRIST " (8). Well—plain fact, as well as pattern for us, this is the tender affection of his part of the fellowship ; later, he will have further opportunity to mention the love on their part. Such is one of the marks of the Good Companions. See next that it is—

A FELLOWSHIP EXPRESSED IN SERVICE

Someone has oddly defined friendship as " Four feet on the fender "—quaint, but surely inadequate, for it is one side of the thing only. Certainly, Christian fellowship is also " Four feet on the road ". Paul's good companions were not just fellows of the armchair—but fellows of the workshop and of the warpath. Their friendship expresses itself in service—to one another, and to the common cause.

That common cause is " the Gospel " (5, 7). Paul and his friends knew this gospel as *a Saving Message*—a life-transforming " good news ". Up against the bad news of their sinnership came this good news of CHRIST's saviourhood. Like in the old pre-war days, boys and men would parade the streets selling their newspapers with their placards of big events before them, so Paul had arrived in Philippi with the good news, as he says in writing Galatians iii. 1 (Gk.) " before whose eyes JESUS CHRIST hath been placarded among you as crucified ". In those days a magistrate placarded his proclamation in a public spot that an execution had taken place—as, indeed, is done outside the prison in like circumstances to-day. So this apostle preached CHRIST crucified to these people, who had turned from their sin, and taken Him for their Saviour, and trusted Him for all. Thus they found this gospel " the power [Gk., ' dynamite ' ; blowing them right side up] of GOD unto salvation ", Romans i. 16—a saving message.

Straight away they conceived this " gospel " as *a Serving Ministry*—they could not now deny it to the world that needed it so much, even as they themselves had previously done. How intrigued they would have been with the story of the four lepers in II Kings vii. 3, who, regaling themselves with the surprising blessing of " bread enough and to spare ", Luke xv. 17, suddenly realised their responsibility to break the news to other starving souls, " We do not well : this day is a day of good tidings [a gospel day], and we hold our peace ". So was it with these Philippian converts. To quote Dr. Plummer, " every convert had become a missionary " ; right from the start, " from the

first day " (5), and their enthusiasm showed no sign of waning,
" until now ", they had demonstrated that their fellowship with
Paul, their gospel-bringer, was that each of them should be a
gospel-bearer to others. The apostle himself had lost no time in
enlisting for this glorious adventure ; for immediately following
upon his conversion, Acts ix. 20, records of him that " straightway
he preached CHRIST in the synagogues ". Does all this condemn
us—that we have been so shy, so scared, so slow to speak the
word for Him ?

These first European believers soon discovered, however, that
this happy fellowship in the gospel involved *a Suffering Member-
ship*—they would not have the easy, comfortable time that most
of us have. They were " partakers of my grace " (7), and it was
as well, for they were henceforth committed to a life spent in
the " defence " negatively, or in the " confirmation ", positively,
of the gospel—all which, in the conditions and circumstances in
which they found themselves, might so easily lead to " bonds ".
Paul's own proclamation of the gospel in their city had brought
him to that fearful, fœtid " inner prison ", Acts xvi. 24, after
the cruel suffering of scourging. Yet, how well worth while the
apostle would have declared it to be, seeing what mighty results
followed. Indeed, one of the contributing factors to those results
was the joy of the two good companions who mingled their
prayers with their praises, thanking GOD that they were counted
worthy to suffer for His Name. They were like the Psalmist
who, though speaking of " my sore in the night ", speaks also of
" my song in the night ", Psalm lxxvii. 2, 6. Ah, it was the
Master Himself " Who, for the joy that was set before Him,
endured the cross, despising the shame ", Hebrews xii. 2. And
we, as co-inheritors with Him, as Romans viii. 17 explains, " if
so be that we suffer with Him, that we may be also glorified
together." We shall look further into this part of the " fellowship " when we come to study iii. 10 of this Epistle. Meanwhile
we turn now to consider this blessed partnership as—

A Fellowship irradiated by Hope

It is a noteworthy thing that Christianity is the only religion
that has this quality of hope. It is not found with the Buddhist,
whose keynote is pessimism, and whose longing is to fade away
into the forgetfulness of nirvana. It is not found with the
Mohammedan, whose characteristic is fatalism. In striking
contrast, the Christian faith is shot through with this thread of
unconquerable and radiant hope.

It is *an assured hope*—" being confident of this very thing " (6) :
the confidence resting on what " He " is to do, not on what we
are to do—He, not we, is ever the main emphasis of the New
Testament. Be it remembered that, in the New Testament, hope
is not something that we have not got, but hope we may get ;
it is something that we have not got yet, but know we shall get
eventually. Such a confidence is begotten in the apostle's mind
concerning the fulfilment of GOD's purpose in the heart and life
of the believer. The reader is taken back to the beginning of
things—" He . . . . hath begun a good work in you ". Our
conversion day, our moment of regeneration, was the start.
When Lydia heard this Epistle read in the church, how her mind
would travel to her riverside experience three or four years
before. When the gaoler, sitting that day in the same congregation, listened to the words, how his heart leapt at the recollection
of the never-to-be-forgotten episode—the years between had not
dimmed the glory of that night light. When was your beginning
—His beginning in you ? Well now, that start is the guarantee
of the finish—" He . . . . will perform it." You may be very
slow, very refractory, very difficult, but in spite of all that we
may be quite " confident " that he never drops anything half-
done. He leaves no " unfinished symphony ". The commence-
ment is the surety of the continuation until the completion. He
who lays the foundation stone may be relied upon to lay the coping
stone. What a glorious hope it is—resting not on ourselves, nor
on anything that we do, but entirely on Him.

It is *an advent hope*—" until the day of JESUS CHRIST ". I
find it so interesting that so often, when Christian hope is mentioned, it is linked up with what Titus ii. 13 calls " the blessed
[happy] hope " ; and I John iii. 3 says " he that hath this hope
in him [Gk., set upon Him] purifieth himself "—again, it is the
Advent Hope. Commenting on this phrase in our passage,
Lightfoot says, " the expression implies something more than
a temporal limit. The idea of a testing is prominent . . . prepared to meet the day of trial ". Such a test does await every
Christian, after being called up to meet Him, I Thessalonians iv.
16–7, when " every man's work [that is, every Christian man's
work] shall be made manifest . . . of what sort [not what size]
it is ", I Corinthians iii. 13. That is, of course, not a judgment
of sin, as in Revelation xx. 11–5, but an assessment of works.
Since our conversion, when the work began, how have we been
getting on ? Have we been improving in holiness, increasing in
service ? How about our spiritual temperature—has it run down
to cold, is it just now at the unpalatable degree of tepid, Revela

tion iii. 16, or does it keep up to boiling-point ? Opportunities
have opened out before us : have we seen them, and seized them ?
" Occupy till I come ", Luke xix. 13, said the departing Master
to us ; how have we done, will the returning Master enquire.
Well—if, by the twin rules of Trust and Obey, we are allowing
Him to control us and our lives, the assessment will be " thou
good servant ". Of His sovereign grace, He began it—by our
yieldedness, Romans vi. 13, He has been able to continue it—
and, by His love and power, He will assuredly finish it, and
" present you faultless ", Jude 24, at " the day of JESUS CHRIST ".
One last thing about the good companions, it is—

A FELLOWSHIP KNIT BY PRAYER

As we tread the gospel road together, we take hold of their
arm in affection ; and we take hold of GOD for them in supplication. Both these relationships—the affection and the supplication—were so natural to Paul : again and again they are seen
in his fellowship especially with his beloved converts.

With some of them, his prayer is weighted with burden—their
need is so great, their progress is so disappointing. With these
Philippians it is all so different. His prayer for them arises in
sheer " joy " (4). They are journeying to heaven along the
Joy Way : and even their friends' prayers breathe the happy
atmosphere. Every time he thinks of them (3), he thanks GOD
for the way they have turned to Him, for the way they are growing
in grace, and, no doubt, for the way in which they have always
been so ready to minister to his physical necessities. So, in this
delightful fashion, thanksgiving and joy are blended with his
intercession. Just what he asks for them we shall see in our
next chapter, for the verses 9–11 set it out before us. And remember that, as Emerson said, " Your solicitude may do much
or those you love, but your prayers will do more."

WHAT A HAPPY PRAYER !

PHILIPPIANS i. 9–11

" THIS I pray "—the character and content of Paul's prayers form a great stimulus and education in the blest employ. See here—

A PRAYER FOR THE HEART

" *That your love may abound yet more and more in knowledge and in all judgment* " (9). Love is the first of all Christian characteristics, and so the apostle makes that the first of his desires for them—even as he opens with it the catalogue of Christian virtues, " the fruit of the SPIRIT is love . . . .", Galatians v. 22—as though to imply that if that is right, all else will probably fall into its due place. The word translated " abound " signifies " overflow "—a like conception to that of Malachi iii. 10, " prove Me now herewith said the LORD of HOSTS if I will not open you the windows of heaven, and pour you out [such] a blessing, that there shall be not room enough to receive " : all you can do is to overflow it. Or, as the Master said, in John vii. 38, " He that believeth on Me . . . out of [him] shall flow rivers of living water "—verse 37 was the inflow ; iv. 14 was the upflow ; this verse 38 is the overflow. What a grand thought it is that any one of us Christians—yes, any one of us—can overflow with love : an overflowing " with all " love towards GOD, and a selfless love toward our fellows, Matthew xxii. 37–9. Of course, this same writer knew the secret of this so desirable quality, that " the love of GOD is shed abroad in our hearts by the HOLY GHOST, who is given unto us ", Romans v. 5.

It is surprising how such love begets " knowledge "—and that, here, not simply a superficial knowledge, for, in the Greek, an intensive preposition is conjoined with the usual verb, to give it the force of a deep knowledge. Real love for a person brings us rare insight and understanding of them : we see it even in the highest realm—" everyone that loveth . . . knoweth GOD " I John iv. 7. The converse is also true : that if love produces knowledge, knowledge safeguards love. Dr. Plummer has said that " love may go grievously astray—misty thought, emotional conduct, and indiscriminate good nature are perilous ". If this is the point of this passage, which I beg leave to doubt, then this " knowledge " and this " judgment " would be as the banks of love's river, keeping the rushing water within bounds. In this sense, a deepening knowledge of others through experience, a heightening knowledge of GOD through communion, a widening knowledge of truth through the Word, are so greatly to be desired, and to be prayed for. Many of the commentators approve of this latter interpretation of the passage ; but others offer the former explanation for the reader's consideration, which, with great temerity, I venture to endorse. Of this, however, we shall have no quarrel, that both deep knowledge, and overflowing love, are of exceeding worth, and that each, whatever be the meaning here, has a contribution to make toward the perfection of the other—for this twofold blessing let us all pray : whether for ourselves, or for others, as Paul did for his Philippians.

A further qualification of this all-out love is this quality of " all judgment ". Discernment, or insight, is the meaning of this word—a quick, sensitive perception such as would prevent love from doing, saying, thinking the wrong thing. You remember that promise concerning Messiah, in Isaiah xi. 3, that the " SPIRIT of the LORD . . . shall make him of quick understanding ", where the A.V. margin renders it, " of quick scent ". A spiritual sense of smell is of great importance, and is both beneficial to love, and bestowed by love. Barnabas possessed it to an unusual degree. If I may put it thus crudely, he had a nose for the fragrance of the good—recall how he detected that in Saul of Tarsus, when everybody else was afraid of him, Acts ix. 26-7 ; and how he detected it at Antioch, Acts xi. 22-3 ; and how he detected it in John Mark, in spite of that young man's desertion, Acts xv. 37-9. Happy they who have a quick scent for the fragrance of grace : there are many still of the Barnabas ilk ! There are others who have a nose for the effluvium of the evil, who can detect fake doctrines, false notions, and what not. They can exercise a very useful office in the church—as Paul himself did, when he smelt heresy even in Peter, Galatians ii. 11-3 : which, incidentally, Barnabas failed to detect (verse 13). But that great man had not much of a nose for bad smells, but for good ! Of course, I have Scriptural authority for speaking thus of a spiritual nose. In I Corinthians xii., Paul speaks of those who are, as it were, spiritual feet, spiritual hands, spiritual ears, spiritual eyes ; and though he shrinks from naming some as nasal men, he does imply their existence in his phrase, " If the whole were hearing, where were the smelling ? " (verse 17). Let it be freely acknowledged that, in the course of the centuries, the Church has had reason to be grateful for her spiritual noses—men like Athanasius and Luther. But, listen—Paul's prayer proceeds—

A Prayer for the Mind

" *That ye may approve things that are excellent* " (10). According to Lightfoot (and what greater, more painstaking, and more exact scholar shall we follow ?), commenting on the R.V. margin, " things that differ ", it is not " things which are opposed ", for it requires no keen moral sense to discriminate between these, but " things that transcend "—we may add, not between what is good, and what is bad ; but between what is good, and what is better. The word " approve " here means " discriminate "— to test, and set the seal of approval on the one thing rather than on the other. It is akin to the quality of " judgment ", or " discernment " that we discussed in the previous verse.

This is, as we saw, indeed a gift of the Spirit, and must needs be prayed for. Shall I serve God, or not ? The answer needs no wisdom : it is plain to every Christian. Shall I serve God at home, or overseas ? The answer to this may, for various reasons, be hard to see—the believer can serve God anywhere ; but he can serve Him to the best only in one place, the place of His own choosing. How important, therefore, to be able to discriminate. As we get to know Him better, to know His Word more, we shall increasingly possess this gift of discrimination—recognising, of course, the distinction between good and not good ; but also between good and better. How precious is that word in I Corinthians ii. 16, " We have the mind of Christ ". Coming down to the practicalities of ordinary everyday life this touches upon our choice of friends, of books, of amusements, of employments, of ambitions.

Of course, the highest office of this gift of discrimination is to guide us about what would best please and honour God—and what would displease and grieve Him. A gang of boys were bent on doing something wrong, and when one of them demurred, the others twitted him, " Ah, you're afraid that if your father knew he'd hurt you ! " But said he, " No, I am only afraid that if he found out I should hurt him ". Such is " the fear of the Lord . . . the beginning of wisdom ", Proverbs i. 7. That is how it is to be with the children of God : to distinguish between what would hurt, and what would please, the Heavenly Father, and to choose accordingly. That, for Paul's Philippians, and for us, is the happy way of life. The prayer goes on—

A Prayer for the Character

"*That ye may be sincere and without offences till the day of Christ.*" (10). Here is one's character, as it were, in three dimensions. (*a*) As concerns ourselves—"sincere". Apparently adopting the suggestion of some scholars that the word translated "sincere" derives from a word meaning "sunlight", the late Dr. Meyer has this interesting illustration, "Just as the X-rays passing through the limb will at once show the fracture, or the result of some accident, so the X-rays of GOD's truth are always searching the heart. . . . and the man who lives in love does not mind meeting the searching rays of GOD's truth, which show that he is no hypocrite". The idea is, that in His sight we are to be adjudged true, pure, unsullied, whole. In the Authorised Version of I Peter ii. 2 you have "the sincere milk of the Word" —but there the Greek word is different, and means "unadulterated". The idea is, again, the same : true, pure, unmixed with incompatible ingredients. The Child of GOD, as the Word of GOD, is to be entirely wholesome, and wholly devoid of any mixture of inconsistency. Which of us stands the test ? Not by the standard of our own opinion of ourselves—not by the standard of what others think of us—but by the infallible eye of GOD. Do you remember Dr. James Stalker's sermon on "The Four Men"—(1) The Man the World sees ; (2) The Man our Friends see ; (3) The Man we Ourselves see ; (4) The Man GOD sees. The same man ; but only the last is the Real Man.

> "O wad some power the giftie gie us
> To see oursel's as others see us"

sings the Scottish bard ; but how much more salutary that we should see what GOD thinks of us—and then, humbly and prayerfully, to seek to be utterly sincere, through and through.

A further facet of character is, as I think, in the apostle's prayer for these his children in the faith. I Timothy i. 2 (*b*) As concerns others—"without offence". I have the authority of the scholars for holding that the word can with equal accuracy be said to be either intransitive, as in Acts xxiv. 16, "I exercise myself to have always a conscience void of offence . . .", or transitive, as in I Corinthians x. 32, "Give none offence". Here in this context we must decide whether the "offence", or "stumbling", is—stumbling ourselves, or causing others to stumble. Either meaning is legitimate ; and perhaps we may escape the dilemma by ruling that both are referred to. Yet, I cannot help feeling that it is the latter that Paul has in mind in interceding for his friends. He would have them so walk that they shall leave no stumbling-block in the way of others ; even as the writer of Hebrews xii. 13 exhorts his readers, " Make straight paths for your feet, lest that which is lame be turned out of the way ". It is so easy for us to become unmindful of others, and of our influence, for good or ill, upon them. Happy is the Christian who, neither by demeanour nor behaviour, gives anyone the reason, or the excuse, to think wrongly of the faith, or to act wrongly regarding the Master.

That leads me to the third aspect of character (c) As concerns our Saviour—" till the day of CHRIST ". The American scholar, Professor Marvin Vincent, suggests that " till " should rather be rendered " with a view to ". Have you heard of employees, in factories or offices, who work with an eye on the clock ? Well, it is the Christian's joy and wisdom to work with an eye on the Coming. Paul has the same conception in his letter to Titus (ii. 11–3), " The grace of GOD that bringeth salvation hath appeared . . . teaching us that, denying ungodliness and worldly lusts, we should live soberly [concerning ourselves], righteously [concerning others], and godly [concerning our GOD], in this present world ; looking for that blessed hope. . . ." That's it : " we should live . . . looking ". Here is a little girl whose Daddy is returning home after a long term of military service abroad. Mother has received the message that he is on his way —not sure quite when he is to arrive, but it might be almost any day now. The child can scarcely sleep for excitement. Anyhow, she is careful to be clean and spruce those days ; she sees that her bedroom is left neat and tidy ; she is ever so good in all her behaviour ; she rushes home quick as soon as school is over—why all this ? Only that she is living with an eye on the Coming ! So does the keen Christian want to be ready for His arrival—" and not be ashamed before Him at His coming ", I John ii. 28. This happy looking will prove a great stimulus to his holy living. See now how this great intercession concludes with—

A PRAYER FOR THE LIFE

" *Being filled with the fruits of righteousness, which are by* JESUS CHRIST, *unto the glory and praise of* GOD." (11). The character will inevitably issue in conduct. That is why there are plums on those trees in my garden : that is their character coming out in conduct—they are plum trees. That is why those people behave in a Christian manner : it is their character emerging into the open—they are Christians. This last petition of Paul's is exactly parallel to the word in Isaiah lxi. 3, " that they might be called trees of righteousness [" being filled with the fruits of righteousness ", here], the planting of the Lord [" which are by JESUS CHRIST ", here], that He might be glorified [here, " unto the glory and praise of GOD "].

The roots are all right ; for, as the apostle reminded these Philippian believers at the outset (i. 1), they are " in CHRIST "— and if we may reverently put it so, a Soul in such Soil has every chance to flourish : to fail is somehow, somewhere, entirely his own fault. " My Beloved hath a vineyard in a very fruitful hill ", says Isaiah v. 1 : why then should it produce only " wild grapes ", sour grapes ?

The fruits, then, are " in ", and also " by " JESUS CHRIST. He plants the tree, preserves the tree, prunes the tree, that it may bring forth " fruit . . . more fruit . . . much fruit ", John xv. 2, 8. " Herein is My Father glorified ", added the Master ; " that He might be glorified ", said the Isaiah lxi passage ; " unto the glory and praise of GOD ", as Paul says here. We cannot forbear quoting II Thessalonians i. 10, " when He shall come to be glorified in His saints, and to be admired in all them that believe . . . in that day ". Yes, perfectly so in that " day of CHRIST " : why not, then, in measure, in these days that intervene ? For it is not we, but He that is to do it ; " the fruit of the SPIRIT . . .", as Galatians v. 22 reminds us. Ours but to trust and obey ; His to employ His beautiful agencies of fruitfulness in the believer—the rain (Psalm lxviii. 9), the dew (Hosea xiv. 5), the wind (John iii. 8), the sun (Malachi iv. 2). Let us, then, never forget that there is no glory to us in all this. Paul, elsewhere, utterly repudiates any such suggestion : " They glorified GOD in me," Galatians i. 24.

This, then, is the apostle's prayer—in all its fulness and sweetness. We close by repeating our title for this study, What a happy prayer !

THE HAPPINESS OF A HUMBLE SPIRIT

PHILIPPIANS i. 12–26

THE apostle's name, Paul, Paulos, means " little " ; and it seems, according to the first or second century book, *Acts of Paul and Thecla*, which has a description of him, that his name is physically apt. Small in bodily frame yet he was intellectually a giant—yet he was the most humble-minded of men. " The highest degree of the hardest grace ", as Coventry Patmore calls humility. When he speaks of his life so dramatically changed, he takes no credit to himself—" By the grace of GOD I am what I am " ; when he speaks of his life so dynamically charged, he accounts for it as—" not I but the grace of GOD which was with me ", I Corinthians xv. 10. He sums it all up as " not I but CHRIST . . . in me ", Galatians ii. 20. Indeed, he even goes so far as to describe himself as " chief " in sinnership, I Timothy i. 15. Of course, anybody could say all this in false humility : it is in unconscious ways, in undesigned coincidence, that the reality of it all becomes apparent. This is what is beautifully disclosed in the passage that we are now to consider. Here is a man of such obvious importance, and seemingly indispensable—yet he appears to regard himself as one who didn't matter—

SO LONG AS THE GOSPEL WAS FURTHERED

One of this man's passions was " the gospel " (12). In ringing tones he declares, " I am not ashamed of the gospel of CHRIST ", Romans i. 16 ; and he unfolds the reasons why he was not ashamed, in the use of those four " for's " in verses 16–8—(1) " For " the People it serves : Roman, Jew, Greek, so universal in its range. (2) " For " the Power it shows : the dynamite (Gk.) of GOD : not to destruction, but to salvation, " turning right side up ", not as Acts xvii. 6. (3) " For " the Problem it solves : the way in which God can righteously exercise His love in saving us. (4) " For " the Pardon it secures : instead of " the wrath of GOD ", for all who turn and trust Him. All which the gospel does for believers ; and such glorious effects endow Paul's message with a quality for which he can never be ashamed. No wonder that, in I Corinthians ix. 16, he says, " Woe is unto me if I preach not the gospel ". He is a glad man to have such a message to carry : if he were to fail to do that he would be not merely a sad man, but a bad man. He would be guilty of such an iniquity as nearly attached to those four lepers in II Kings vii. 9, " We do not well : this day is a day of good tidings [a gospel day], and we hold our peace ". But enough of this pessimistic side of the matter. Paul did proclaim that gospel ; he rejoiced in it, gloried in it—whatever happened to him.

This inveterate and intrepid missionary roamed hither and thither on his gospel crusade, and, Christian strategist that he was, he ever tried to get an entrance for the Saving Word in the populous, and significantly important, cities of his world—to adopt the late Archbishop Harrington Lees' nomenclature : Corinth, the gospel in a heathen port ; Galatia, the gospel in the country districts ; Ephesus, the gospel in a heathen cathedral city ; Philippi, the gospel in a Roman colony ; Colossae, the gospel in an out-station ; Thessalonica, the gospel in an independent state. Ah, but Rome—if only he could take that gospel to Rome, the Imperial City, the then hub of the universe ! So, in Acts xix. 21 he says, " After I have been there [Jerusalem], I must also see Rome " ; and in Acts xxiii. 11, the LORD assures him, " Be of good cheer, Paul : for as thou hast testified of Me in Jerusalem, so must thou bear witness also at Rome ". Now he is actually there ; but how differently from what he had supposed—he is a prisoner : " my bonds " (13) : yet, as ever, he is a preacher. Nothing will stop him telling out the good news.

To a man of Paul's restless, roving disposition, this incarceration, however mild, must have been an irksome trial. His circumstances were all against him ; but he had long formed the habit of turning opposition into opportunity—and now he is at it again. The indignity, the suffering, the restriction, and the rest : of what consequence were they, if only they could be over-ruled, and made the occasion of furthering the gospel—that, and not he, was what mattered (12). How fared the situation, then, in that Roman house of detention ? (i) " *The palace* "— the word will include the whole soldiery of Cæsar forming the prætorian guard. Paul would all the time be chained at the wrist to one of these military men, who would be relieved in constant succession, and who would go out on the conclusion of their term of guard duty to tell the tale of this remarkable prisoner who, rather than succumbing to his misfortunes, was happily spending his time preaching, and praying, and penning a deal of correspondence. Something of the picture is in Acts xxvii. 30-1. Thus it happened that, as he says, " My bonds in CHRIST are manifest in all the palace " (13), that is, as Lightfoot paraphrases, " have been seen in their relation to CHRIST, have borne testimony to the gospel ". The spread of this influence would be rapid and wide and effective, so that at the end of this very Epistle (iv. 22) Paul is able to speak of " the saints . . that are of Cæsar's household "—an expression that might include the highest functionaries and the lowest menials. Truly, " the things which happened unto [him] have fallen out rather unto the furtherance of the gospel " (12)—he would never have got into this close circle with his message, if he had not been a prisoner ! As the late Bishop T. W. Drury said, " The very chain which Roman discipline riveted on the prisoner's arm secured to his side a hearer who would tell the story of patient suffering for CHRIST among those who, the next day, might be in attendance on Nero himself ".

A further blessing, as it seemed to Paul, accrued to his imprisonment. (ii) " The brethren "—his fellow-Christians in the city caught the infection of his courage. At least " many " of them did (14). Some, as is always the case in any company of Christians, were too fearful to come right out for GOD ; but many here were so deeply stirred by the example and exhortation of this great soul that they waxed confident in spirit and bold in speech. If courage breeds cowardice in some, be assured that it begets confidence in many. Here, too, then, was another influence for GOD directly attributable to " my bonds ". But Paul was suffering from all the inhibitions of his confined condition. Well, what of it ? In modern jargon, he " couldn't care less ". What did he matter, so long as the gospel had " free course ", II Thessalonians iii. 1.

Let us, at least, take this lesson to heart, ere we pass on : that wherever we find ourselves, and whatever our circumstances, there is opportunity for service ; that however we may be hindered and hampered by our conditions, there is some opening for testimony—and that all the more effectual as it is to be seen that we refuse to undergo our trials, but resolve to overcome them. How Paul would have hated our all-too-frequent use of the phrase, " under the circumstances " ! He never allowed them to get on top of him—" in the circumstances ", of course ; but not " under " them. Let us now proceed further, and note his readiness to subdue and subjugate self.

So LONG AS THE SAVIOUR WAS GLORIFIED

" *Christ is preached* " (18)—that is the main thing. If it was not always just as Paul liked, if sometimes the phraseology, or even the doctrine, was a bit unorthodox, if, with some, the motive was not pure, still he rejoiced that anyhow the Name was proclaimed. The Judaisers, who were always trying to hamper Paul's ministry, were, alas, moved by feelings of " envy and strife . . . not sincerely " (15–6). In Galatians (i. 6–9) the alternative is the liberty of the gospel, or the bondage of ritualism [Lightfoot's word]—and Paul comes down with all his weight against the latter. In Philippians, here, the choice is an imperfect Christianity, and an unconverted state—and Paul " will rejoice " in the former, in spite of what it lacks of the full Christian truth and the true Christian spirit. On the other hand, there are those who would show their goodwill to the captive preacher (15)— who, while the others would add gall to his bonds, would bring gladness to his heart. These latter recognise that he is " set for the defence of the gospel " (17)—posted as a sentry, is the Moffatt Commentary's interpretation of " set ". He is not caring over much for his own defence ; but he does care intensely that the gospel shall suffer no inroads of false interpretation. If he had not stood for the proclamation of the pure gospel, he would never have been in bonds : seeing he is thus, he will not relax his watchfulness. He is glad that CHRIST is preached any way ; but his great concern is that He shall be preached in all His sole and unique grandeur. What a faithful sentry this " good soldier of JESUS CHRIST ", II Timothy ii. 3, had always been, challenging every movement, and every man, " Who goes there—friend or foe ? "

" *Christ shall be magnified* " (20)—is Paul's ambition : not himself, but his Saviour. How his heart would glow if he heard John the Baptist's declaration, " He must increase, but I must decrease ", John iii. 30. Says R. C. Joynt, " Mary's magnificat was ' My *soul* doth magnify the LORD ' ; St. Paul's, " CHRIST shall be magnified in my *body* "—even as he exhorts those very believers in Rome, from where he writes, " I beseech you, therefore, brethren . . . that ye present your bodies. . . . ", Romans xii. 1. CHRIST magnified in the body—magnified by lips that bear happy testimony to Him ; magnified by hands employed in His happy service ; magnified by feet only too happy to go on His errands ; magnified by knees happily bent in prayer for His Kingdom ; magnified by shoulders happy to bear one another's burdens, and so fulfil the law of CHRIST. So, whether in life, or in death, this body is to be so employed in His service, whether bound or free, that we shall not be ashamed to meet His gaze, nor afraid to be bold in His cause (20).

There are two kinds of magnification : (i) That of *the Microscope*—that makes the little seem big. With this the Christian has nothing to do, for there is nothing little about his Lord—though, alas, He may have but little place in a Christian's life ; and " no room " at all with the worldling. (ii) That of *the Telescope*—that makes the really big loom big. The vessel may appear as a dot on the horizon ; but this instrument brings it out in its true proportions. Or, if you like, it brings the distant near. That is the Christian's joy : his body and being becoming a telescope, showing to others His true greatness, and bringing to those who see Him but far off the sense of His real nearness. When the Psalmist moves the proposition, " O magnify the Lord with me ", Psalm xxxiv. 3, and when Paul seconds the resolution, " CHRIST shall be magnified " — it is this latter ministry that is in mind. Shall we carry it out unanimously ? Thus, once again, we observe that Paul is thinking, wishing, nothing for himself—

So long as the Others are Helped.

There is a choice before his mind—" to live . . . to die " (21). *If he is to consult his own interest*—he has no hesitation in coming to a decision : " to die is gain ". What is it to die ? Paul tells us it is (*a*) " to depart "—a metaphorical word, suggestive of a nautical figure, a loosing of moorings preparatory to setting sail ; or of a military figure, a striking of camp ready to start on the march. He would for himself so gladly do that straight away. In II Timothy iv. 6, when his earthly end really had come, he says, using the same word and metaphor, " the time of my departure is at hand ". The storm-tossed mariner sailing away on the last ocean voyage, to the haven where he would be ; the battle-scarred warrior marching away off the field of war, for his Sovereign's Review—that is the apostle's idea of death, on the one side of it, the negative side. (*b*) " to be with CHRIST " —that is the positive side ; and, by the very words employed, how filled with blest anticipation. Of course, there is a certain, and real sense in which believers are " with CHRIST " now ; indeed, " He that is not with Me is against Me ", Matthew xii. 30. Yet there is a relationship to Him somehow more intimate awaiting us yonder. I wonder if an illustration might successfully convey the difference ? You get to know a certain person, and become friendly. After a bit he invites you to go and stay with him. You greatly enjoy your visit ; but, of course, you return to your own house. However, the ties of friendship are fostered and strengthened, and you become very close to each other, so that one day your friend invites you to go and live with him. Right gladly you leave your own house, so much poorer than his, and on the appointed day you move into his, to share with him the richness, the beauty, the joy of that new lovely home. Does that properly illustrate the difference between the two aspects of this " with CHRIST " ? Our earthly experience a Staying with Him, our heavenly experience a Living with Him. You will naturally recall His own allusion in John xiv. 2, " In My Father's house are many mansions . . . I go to prepare a place for you." How immeasurably " far better " the apostle knows that to be (23).

> " O think ! to step on shore,
> And that shore Heaven ;
> To take hold of a hand,
> And that GOD's hand !
> To breathe a new air !
> And find it celestial air !
> To feel invigorated,
> And to know it Immortality !
>
> O think ! to pass from the storm and the tempest,
> To one unbroken calm ;
> To wake up,
> And find it glory ! "

Yet there is another side. *If he is to consult his converts' interest* —he doubtless must abide awhile with them—" to abide in the flesh is more needful for you " (24). To continue in life would add still more fruit for his labour (22)—yes, but that is not what will decide this matter for him : which is the more profitable for them ? That is the point with this wholly selfless man. If he stay, he would hope to help with the enlargement (" further-ance ") of their faith—he is no believer in a merely static religion, he would have them to be always growing in grace and knowledge, II Peter iii. 18. His staying would also contribute to the enjoyment (" joy ") of their faith—he is so constantly dwelling upon the joy of religion, and especially is he stressing that in this particular Epistle which, written in captivity, might have been supposed to be always striking a note of gloom. He trusts that his visiting them again, as he hopes to do, will cause their " rejoicing " to become " more abundant " (26). So his mind is made up :

he will gladly sink his own personal preference, and, for their sakes, he will be content to " continue " with, and for, them.

The true humility of this man, so unmindful of self-advantage, makes him a man of rich happiness—which the self-centred, self-seeking man can never be.

V

HAPPY WARRIORS

PHILIPPIANS i. 27–ii. 4

" STAND FAST "—" striving together "—" your adversaries "—
" the same conflict." You see, there's a war on. Consider—

THE THING WE FIGHT FOR

"Striving . . . for the faith of the gospel " (27). When writing to the Thessalonian believers (I. ii. 4), Paul says " we were allowed of GOD to be put in trust with the gospel ". Speaking under this military metaphor, it is as if the gospel standard were placed in the hands of the Christian army, to be planted in other lands, and in other lives. That is one of the mighty privileges " allowed " to us believers—privileges, yes, and responsibilities, too. This is what the soldiers would call *a strategic front*—especially with Paul himself always seeking to carry the fight to the points of influential life, and busy traffic, such as this Philippi, and that Thessalonica. It is also a strategic operation when you and I seek to capture one soul by the gospel of JESUS CHRIST, for who, but GOD Himself, can tell what that one may be, or do. Truly, Christian history justifies us in applying to this case the words of Isaiah lx. 22, " A little one shall become a thousand ". Besiege that one, strive for that one—that the gospel flag may be thus far advanced among the kingdom of men.

No one who has ever engaged in this godly manoeuvre will deny that it is *a strenuous front*—this work of soul-winning is no easy matter, for the enemy will concentrate all his forces to prevent, if he can, our taking the city. All that is implied in that word " striving " will be required from us ; all that lies behind the exhortation to " stand fast "—to stand your ground, in face of the foe's counter-attacks—may be called for. Such battles are not normally won simply by the happy little handing of a tract, and the putting up of a simple little prayer—though GOD forbid that I should belittle the immense possibilities of a tract and a prayer. It is only the careless, and almost flippant,

manner in which this is sometimes done that I am warning myself
and you about. Do you remember that verse of Horatius Bonar's

> " Go, labour on while it is day :
>   The world's dark night is hastening on ;
> Speed, speed thy work ; cast sloth away ;
>   It is not thus that souls are won ".

All the modern hymn-books have that last line thus : but in
an earlier day we used to sing it differently, and as I feel sure
was Dr. Bonar's original wording—

> " With strong great wrestlings souls are won ".

How GOD had to wrestle for Jacob's soul—" there wrestled a
Man with him ", Genesis xxxii. 24. It was there, at long last,
at Jabbok, not at Bethel, in chapter xxviii, that the patriarch
was, as we should say, converted. Ay, this planting of the
Flag is not for slothful Christians, but for those who are prepared
for strenuous wrestling.

One further thing we will note as, through the telescope of
this passage, we survey the scene of the spiritual combat : that
it is *a single front*—" in one spirit ", he says, and " with one
mind " ; it is a " striving together " ; and they share " the same
conflict ". One is at one end of the line, Paul at Rome ; others
at the other end, those at Philippi—but it is the same line.
Zephaniah iii. 9 has a beautiful idea in the margin, " to serve Him
with one shoulder ". Have you ever seen a military march-
past ? Not a shoulder out of place : for all the world as if it
were but one shoulder. What a picture of a united front ! There
may be different regiments—call them, if you will, Anglicans,
Congregationalists, Baptists, Brethren, Methodists, Presbyteri-
ans, and so on ; but it is the same army, facing the same enemy,
in the same Cause, under the same Commander, the " Captain
of the host of the LORD ", Joshua v. 14, " the Captain of their
salvation ", Hebrews ii. 10, a Commander to the people ", Isaiah
iv. 4. Uniformity—means wearing the same uniform, which I
don't know that we want ; Unity—means fighting the one cause,
for which CHRIST Himself prayed, " that they all may be one . . .
that the world may believe ", John xvii. 21. Let us, then,
forswear fighting each other, and see that we are found " striving
together for the faith of the gospel ". For, ponder—

THE ENEMY WE FIGHT AGAINST—

" *Your adversaries* " (28). Ah yes, whenever we are seeking
to advance the Flag of the Faith there will be foes who, whether

consciously or unconsciously, are under the direction of the chief enemy of souls—" your adversaries " are the tools and instruments of " your adversary ", I Peter v. 8. All along the line Paul had had painful experience of adversaries—even in this very Philippi, to which he was writing, as Acts xvi. 22-4 tells us. And, inasmuch as he always practised what he preached, he is able authoritatively to exhort these believers to be " in nothing terrified " by the opposition. The word is " scared " —the idea is of a horse shying from sudden fright. So, says the apostle, and he knew what he was talking about, don't shy at anything that the enemy shall do, or threaten—but seek grace from GOD to " stand fast " to your purpose (27). To " suffer " for CHRIST Paul counts as high privilege (30)—indeed, martyrdom was eagerly sought by many believers in those perilous days of the early Church : it is honour " to believe ", it is honour " to suffer ". Like Wordsworth's Happy Warrior, who " Turns his necessity to glorious gain ".

Note what is the effect of such steadfastness upon the enemy —" *which is to them an evident token of perdition* " (28). Such stout resistance in the face of all that their opposition and persecution can do fills them with apprehension. There begins to dawn on them the realisation that the game is up ! " Your adversary, the devil, as a roaring lion, walketh about, seeking whom he may devour ", I Peter v. 8 ; but by faith we may receive the lion-heart of Him who is " the Lion of the tribe of Judah ", Revelation v. 5. This your fearlessness when menaced by persecution will make it quite evident to the foe that victory lies with you : " and that of GOD ". It is not we, but He that overcomes. You may say that the blushing boy David conquers the massive, booming Goliath—but, in reality, it is GOD that does it, as that brave " youth ", I Samuel xvii. 33, was well aware—" this day will the LORD deliver thee into mine hand " (verse 46). Well, how depressing to the enemy is the endurance of the saints. It is time we turned our attention to—

THE SOLDIERS WE FIGHT WITH

We do not fight alone ; as we saw just now, it is a united front —we are members of an army, combating for a common objective. What, then, is to be our relation to our fellows alongside of whom we battle ? What a difference it makes if the fifteen, or eleven, of a football side, or if the members of a cricket team, or if the masters of a school staff, or if the crew of a racing-eight, or if the people of a local church (hence iv. 2), or if the men of an army company, are completely friendly toward each other—

they will work, or strive, or serve, or fight, so much the more happily and successfully. What, then, of the personal relations between the soldiers of the Cross ?

Dropping all metaphor, verses 3–4 of chapter ii. have much of importance to say to us. (i) *There is to be no internal strife—* " of one accord, of one mind "(2) ; " let nothing be done through strife or vainglory ". Quarrelsomeness can do such a lot of damage, and bring such discredit upon the Cause ; yet one does find Christians at loggerheads—and often over such stupid, trifling matters : all too frequently it is concerned with personal grievances and self-glorification. (ii) *There is to be no fancied superiority*—" in lowliness of mind let each esteem others better than themselves ". The Greek word here translated " lowliness of mind " was, according to Lightfoot, always used in a bad sense, meaning abject, grovelling ; but, as the result of the life of CHRIST, this quality of humility is, in the New Testament, raised to its proper level. There is such a thing as mock-humility, of the Uriah Heep type—true lowliness is so different from this. Let us not forget that there is also a true and proper pride—a sense of the honour of being in such an Army. Listen to Paul in Acts xxvii. 23, " GOD whose I am, and whom I serve " : with what ringing tones the words are uttered, reflecting his feeling of privilege. It does not spring from any idea of his own worthiness, or achievement, but is the expression of his realisation of the wonder of his Commander. Concerning himself, and relating to others, his attitude is always to be humble-spirited. (iii) *There is to be no self-seeking*—" look not every man on his own things, but every man also on the things of others ". That word " look " is an unusual one. It means to regard fixedly, so as to aim at. See that man at the butts : how carefully his eye is on that bull, all his attention and concern is on it. So is it with some people that they are so exclusively occupied with their own interests that they are entirely oblivious of anyone else's. To be for ever looking for, scheming for, his own self-advantage is the mark of a thoroughly bad soldier. See where it lead that unfortunate soldier, Achan, in Joshua vii. 9. When he saw the gold, the silver, and the garment he thought at once of his own enrichment, with not a thought of what it would entail for his family, and for his fellow-soldiers. Let the Christian warrior take warning. We pass on to think of—

THE LEADERS WE FIGHT UNDER

We have here *a moving glimpse of the Human Leader*. Paul had meant so much to that church at Philippi, since the day when he crossed over to the city from Troas ; he had shown such constant care of them ; he held them in special affection ; they were joined with him in such an inspiring comradeship—" having the same conflict which ye saw in me [when he was beaten and imprisoned in their city], and now hear to be in me [imprisoned in Rome] ", i. 30. I am sure that on his next visit he would have chosen, if it had then been extant, as his opening hymn, " Blest be the tie that binds our hearts in Christian Love ". It is grand when we can rejoice over those who, under GOD, have been our human leaders. How the present writer thanks GOD for the vicar of his boyhood's church, the late Archdeacon R. C. Joynt, and for two vicars under whom he served as curate, the Rev. A. Cochrane, and Canon W. E. Daniels—and so many others, his " elders and betters " in the LORD. Ah yes, it is good to have leaders whom we can esteem and revere. But, says Paul, you must not depend too much on them—" whether I come and see you, or else be absent ", you are to " stand fast " : your feet founded not on him, but on Him.

So we get here *a clear view of the Divine Leader*. " In one Spirit " —the One SPIRIT. " For by One SPIRIT are we all baptised into one body . . . and have been all made to drink into One SPIRIT ", I Corinthians xii. 13 ; " For through Him we both have access by One SPIRIT unto the Father ", Ephesians ii. 18. Yes, He is our Leader, for " as many as are led by the SPIRIT of GOD, they are the sons of GOD ", Romans viii. 14. Does your watch keep good time ? I have a hall-clock, which is a great friend of mine ; it was presented to me when I left my first curacy, in 1918. Its only trouble is that it is, in its old age, a bad time-keeper. In my constant attempts to keep it right I am driven to seek a guide. Where shall I look for such leadership ? Ah, my watch ! No, alas ; for while the clock always loses, my watch always gains. You will guess that it is my regular habit to regulate both by TIM—the telephone automatic recording of Greenwich Mean Time. Learn, then, to go for leadership, not to those who, even the best of them, may go wrong, and lead you astray, but to the fountain head—to the SPIRIT of GOD Himself—not human leadership, but Divine, whether in life's wayfare, or life's warfare.

The story is told that in the French Wars our soldiers were very dispirited on the eve of a great battle, owing to the disparity in the number of the English troops. Gathered around a camp fire as night fell a few men were pessimistically discussing the situation ; every now and then another, and another, joined the group, unrecognised in the darkness, but all seemed to agree on the hopelessness of the morrow's fight : they were so heavily outnumbered—their own so few, the enemy's so many. When out spoke a new voice in the discussion—a voice of one who had come unnoticed in the shadows of the fire-light—a voice so well-known to them all—a voice whose ringing tones called them instantly out of their despair—a voice that posed one strategic question : " And how many do you count *me* for ? " It was the Iron Duke himself, the great Duke of Wellington, who led them that next morning, in spite of the French big majority, to a brilliant victory. How much, how many, do you count your Leader for ? If you are even standing alone for Him in the fight—in your office, in your workshop, in your factory, in your school, in your company, in your home—remember the blessed truth that " One, with GOD, is always a majority ". Even if there be but two of you, and that, surrounded by belligerent forces, II Kings vi. 16 remains true, " Fear not, for they that be with us are more than they that be with them ". Such, O ye Philippians, O ye my readers, is the Leader under whom this fight of faith is waged to victory. And now—

THE UNIFORM WE FIGHT IN

Qualities of Christian character are, in the Epistles, so often likened to articles of clothing, and pieces of armour, that I make no apology for treating our closing meditation under that suggestive figure. Look, first, at i. 27, " Only let your conversation [behaviour] be as becometh the gospel of CHRIST ". It would be altogether unbecoming for you to fight your country's battles in the enemy's uniform ; so should we, as Christians, be careful to " put off " the old clothes, or habits, of sin, and to " put on " the new garments of godliness, Ephesians iv. 22–5. " As becometh . . . ." (a) the gospel of love, " See that ye love one another with a pure heart fervently ", I Peter i. 22 ; (b) the gospel of peace, " Follow peace with all ", Hebrews xii. 14 ; (c) the gospel of power, " Let not sin reign in your body ", Romans vi. 12 ; (d) the gospel of heaven, " Love not the world ", I John ii. 15 ; (e) the gospel of GOD, " Be ye therefore followers of GOD, as dear children ", Ephesians v. 1. Strange dress, do you think, for the military scene ; yet this is the uniform in which CHRIST's soldiers fight best, and which the foe fears most.

Come to ii. 1–2. Paul has here a fourfold argument for their rejoicing his heart by appearing in just such a uniform of Christly character as we have been examining. " If there be any consolation in CHRIST "—if your experience of Him is any encouragement

to you; " if any comfort of love "—if love exerts any
persuasive power with you; " if any fellowship of the SPIRIT "
—if that fellowship with Him is a reality; " if any bowels and
mercies "—if you have affectionate yearnings of heart.   On
these grounds " fulfil ye my joy ".   There he goes again : he
can't keep Joy out of it.   In this brief Epistle he mentions this
characteristic under various words, no less than nineteen times
—almost five times for every chapter.   " My scrip of joy, immortal diet ", as Sir Walter Raleigh called it.   Dr. Lightfoot
has a beautiful paraphrase of this " fulfil ye my joy ".   He renders
it, " you have given me joy hitherto.   Now fill my cup of gladness
to overflowing ".

So Paul sums up the uniform in the words, " having the same
love ".   When he writes to urge the Colossian Christians to don
the uniform, he finishes by saying, " Above all these things put
on love ", Colossians iii. 14—as if love were the overcoat, the
cloak, covering, protecting, beautifying all else.   What joy it
will give this old warrior to watch these young soldiers marching
forth to the Philippian battle-ground o'erclad with love.   As
the familiar hymn says—

> " Let your drooping hearts be glad ;
> March in Heavenly armour clad."

That armour is so different from earth's—its girdle is truth, its
breastplate is righteousness, its sandals is peace, its shield is
faith, its helmet is salvation, its sword is Scripture, its greaves
is prayer, Ephesians vi. 14–18.   Just the kind of things we here
have spoken of.

VI

RUNGS OF GLADNESS

PHILIPPIANS ii. 5–11

WHEN old Jacob saw his dream ladder, in Genesis xxviii. 12, he found the angels of GOD ascending and descending on it—as if carrying up the news of his needs, and coming down with his supplies to meet them. Our LORD uses the story of the ladder as a picture of Himself, John i. 51—through whom our requests mount up to GOD ("in My Name," John xv. 16), and through whom His answers of supply reach us ("by CHRIST JESUS", Philippians iv. 19). Those were Ladders of Communication —whereon our great need and His great fulness meet. Now, in our present passage, we have, as it were, another ladder, a Ladder of Consecration—whereby man's greatest, deepest need is met eternally, because of the Princely mercy and Sovereign grace of GOD. For all the simplicity of most of its words, it is, in very truth, one of the most profound passages in the whole of Holy Writ. Let us think it over under this simile of the Glory Ladder, whereon He trod for our redemption—rungs of gladness, indeed, for us ; and for Him, "Who for the joy that was set before Him endureth the cross, despising the shame, and is set down at the right hand of the throne of GOD", Hebrews xii. 2 : back at the topmost rung again.

THE WAY DOWN

Six steps He took, until He reached the lowest depth. We begin at the top, where we see Him as (i) "*Being in the form of* GOD." His was the essential and eternal Being of Deity. He always had been, always would be, GOD : whatever were the conditions and circumstances of His Old Testament appearances (and they were many ; generally under the guise of the Angel of the LORD), Deity always was His. He was the Angel at the Bush, in Exodus iii. 2 : hence the command to Moses to worship. He was the Soldier with the Sword, in Joshua v. 13 : hence the instinctive action of Joshua to worship. Angel Soldier, what not— but always GOD. And when He came down in the New Testament to His incarnation it was the same, He brought His Deity with Him. He never Himself used the title, though He accepted it from others—He called Himself here Son of Man, not Son of GOD : but that essential Deity did not, could not, ever leave Him. It is of fundamental importance that we remember this. Note that He " thought it not robbery to be equal with GOD " —He was not taking to Himself something that did not belong to Him, when He lay claim to be thus " equal " ; nor, as we shall see, did He think it to be something to be clung to, laid hold on, lest He lose it. No, it was of nature His by right. " Making Himself equal with GOD ", John v. 18, was the Jews' disgusted accusation against Him.

So stands our Divine Lord at the top of the Ladder. Watch Him as He prepares to take His first step down—in itself a mighty descent. (ii) *He " made Himself of no reputation "*. Can you imagine a royal personage, wishing to travel incognito, divesting himself of all apparel and appearance that would give him away. He would still be a king, but he would have emptied himself of his royal habitrament. Something thus happened here : He " emptied Himself " is the right rendering of the phrase. I am suggesting that He divested Himself, not of His Deity, but of His glory—stripping Himself of the insignia of His majesty. He never used that Deity for His own benefit, for He would live down here as truly Man—not pretending, nor masquerading, as man, but really so. For all that, flashes of Deity did sometimes emanate from His sacred Person—for instance, on the Mount of Transfiguration, and when, at the arrest in the Garden, the soldiers fell to the ground at His use of the Divine Name, " I am . . .", John xviii. 6. Ah yes, He that thought it not robbery to be equal with GOD, thought it not forgery to use His signature. See Exodus iii. 14. So His glory was laid aside, as Milton's magnificent lines describe it—

> " That glorious Form, that light insufferable
>
> .   .   .   .   .
>
> He laid aside : and here with us to be,
> Forsook the courts of everlasting day,
> And chose with us a darksome house of mortal clay."

It is often said that when He became Man, He subjected Himself to the human liability to error, as the rest of us. I am bound to say that I find it impossible to associate mistakes with Deity. Limitations, yes, voluntarily assumed ; but not errors. I conceive it, therefore, to be the case that whatever He said was always true. At the same time, we must, I think, hold that He suffered Himself to be limited. How else could there be any reality or normality, in His human childhood—what meaning could there be in the words of Luke ii. 52, "and JESUS increased in wisdom . . ."? Yet, I suspect that, even at school, He never actually made mistakes. Do you recall that description of the Child's session with the Temple doctors, "All that heard Him were astonished at His understanding and answers", Luke ii. 47.

So he steps down (iii) He "took upon Him the form of a servant". A bond-slave! To whom? to GOD—"Behold, My servant", Isaiah lii. 13; and, quoting from Psalm xl. 7, "Lo, I come to do Thy will, O GOD", Hebrews x. 7. At the moment when He divested Himself of the apparel of the Son, He donned the apron of the Servant—to GOD; and, as Plummer adds, "perhaps we may say to the whole race of mankind". Yet, it is interesting that, though we are "the bond-slave of JESUS CHRIST" (as Romans i. 1, etc.), He is not said to be the bond-slave of us—in this latter relation, a less harsh, a kindlier Greek word is used. "The Son of Man came not to be ministered unto but to minister", Mark x. 45; "I am among you as He that serveth", Luke xxii. 27. Still, in spite of this distinction of status, we do find Him, at least on one occasion, doing the duty of a bond-slave, when, in John xiii. 4, He "took a towel", to rinse His disciples' feet. Coming in from the dust of the road, the guest at a meal would hold his feet over the earthenware basin, while a slave rinsed them from the water ewer. There was no such slave present, and the guests should, therefore, have done this service for one another; but as they refrained from this menial duty, our Lord Himself did it. And that at a moment when He was acutely aware of His high dignity, "Knowing that the Father had given all things into His hands, and that He was come from GOD, and went to GOD". By the way, isn't this episode a striking illustration in miniature of the use of those first two rungs of the Ladder we are talking of—(a) "He laid aside His garments", as of royal splendour; (b) "He took a towel, and girded Himself," as with the garb of lowly service.

He goes down farther (4) He "was made in the likeness of men." If I remember rightly, the Authorised Version never (except in our verse 8) speaks of our LORD as "a man", but always as "Man", and correctly so—as also the Creed, "and was made Man"—for He was not merely an individual, but the Representative of the Race, the whole of human-kind. He went to the Cross, not as a man merely, but as Man, as all men, "He died for all", II Corinthians v. 15—so that all may, if they will, share in the redemptive benefit. So here, not the likeness of a man, but " of men ". Thus, as we said earlier, He was not here on earth playing at being a man, but was as truly Man as He was truly GOD—a dual truth incomprehensible to our finite mind, but apprehensible to our grateful heart. How we thank GOD for all the Bible evidences of the reality of His manhood—that He was hungry, Matthew iv. 2 ; that He was tempted, Matthew iv. 3 ; that He was tired, Mark iv. 38—" for in that He Himself hath suffered being tempted, He is able to succour them that are tempted ", Hebrews ii. 18 ; indeed, as the previous verse says, " In all things it behoved Him to be like unto His brethren ". When the great railway engineer, George Stephenson, died, his long funeral procession contained a body of plain workmen, who bore a banner inscribed with the words, " He was one of us "—- for he had risen from their ranks. Truly, *He* is one of us—for He came down to join our rank.

What high level of humanity was it that this " Prince of Glory " came to occupy ? Nay, no high level at all (5) " *He humbled Himself* ". Says our hymn, " The highest place that heaven affords, is His, is His, by right " ; yet, on earth, it was a lowly station that He sought—an insignificant village, a humble cottage, a lowly mother, a poor trade. He was born to a borrowed cradle ; He was laid in a borrowed tomb ; and during His ministry " the Son of Man hath not where to lay His head ". It would seem as if this choice of the humble were a principle of selection in all the service of GOD. Recall that passage in I Corinthians i. 26 ff.—" Not many wise . . . not many mighty, not many noble are called " : He does not say " not any ", but not many. Rather has He chosen, " the foolish . . . the weak . . . the base. . . the despised . . . the nonentities, the ' are nots ' ". " Chosen ", mark you. It is not that He has to put up with these inconsiderables as the best He could get ; but deliberately He so frequently prefers such, that people may be forced to recognise that the praise for the results must go, not to the human instruments, but to the hand that uses them. After a battle of long ago, when a soldier had wrought great devastation with his sword, his king sent for the sword. Upon inspection, His Majesty returned it with the somewhat scornful remark, " But it is a very ordinary sword ". To which the soldier ventured to reply, " His Majesty should have sent for the arm that wielded it ". Yes, that's it ; or, to put it differently, " We have this treasure in earthen vessels, that the excellency of the power may be of GOD, and not of us ", II Corinthians iv. 7. But all this is to stray from our immediate subject—the wonderful spirit of humility that He displayed in his lowly station, in His humble service, and in His denial of self. At the end they said, " He saved others, Himself He cannot save ", Matthew xxvii. 42 —how false that latter part, for, by exercise of His Deity, He could at any moment have come down from that Cross—

> " Was it the nails, O Saviour, that bound Thee to the Tree ?
> Nay 'twas Thine everlasting love, Thy love for me, for me."

How true that former part, "others", always others, as He " went about doing good ", Acts x. 38, in the homes of sinners, and in the haunts of lepers.

How moving is this self-humbling of the Holy One and the Mighty. Yet, mark another stage of His descent (6) He " *became obedient unto death* ". What depth for Deity ! Why could He not have been raptured to heaven without dying, as Enoch was, and Elijah ; and as living believers will be at His Parousia, I Thessalonians iv. 17 ? The whole efficacy of redemption lies in His dying. That is a mysterious utterance which we find in Hebrews v. 8-9. " Though He were a Son, yet learned He obedience by the things which He suffered ; and being made perfect, He became the author of eternal salvation unto all them that obey Him ". Anyhow, we may say that part of the meaning is that, by His suffering of death, He showed obedience up to the hilt ! We are back in the majestic argument of Romans v. 19, " For as by one man's disobedience [the] many were made sinners, so by the obedience of One shall [the] many be made righteous ".

Stay a moment ! Think you that He is now at the very bottom of the Ladder of our Salvation ? No ; there is a rung yet. (7) " *Even the death of the Cross* ". See that cross, in its glittering gold, at the very apex of London's St. Paul's Cathedral, shining in religious splendour over the City's busy traffic : not such was it " on which the Prince of Glory died "—but one of rough-hewn wood, a criminal's gibbet, stuck into a hole on Jerusalem's common crucifixion ground. Three of them were there at the time—two of them for a couple of base malefactors, and the middle one intended for the leader of the nefarious gang, one, Bar-abbas ; but now occupied by his Substitute and ours. To that place, to that death, to that depth, His journey from the skies has brought Him—" being nailed to a tree like vermin ", as Plummer says. One thinks of the Psalm that was in His mind as He hung there, and, in reverent reticence, one wonders if He dwelt upon the words, " I am a worm, and no man ; a reproach of men, and despised of the people ", Psalm xxii. 6. GOD—man—worm :

what a far distance down the scale of Being. Says America's
Norman B. Harrison, " History has no parallel. How could He
do it ? Mute in contemplation, we can never cease to wonder ".
Truly, He has now touched bottom. As one stands there, at the
place where one ought to be—

> " Two wonders I confess.
> The wonder of His glorious love,
> And my own worthlessness."

Ah, but GOD did not leave Him there ; and now, with uttermost
joy, we watch His journey to the skies. He grasps once more
the Ladder, and we mark—

THE WAY UP

Wonderful in glory, as the Way Down was wonderful in grace.
Three great steps, and He is back where He properly belongs.
(i) " *Wherefore God also hath highly exalted Him* ". We have seen
that He humbled Himself, but He did not exalt Himself. By
reason of His Deity, He could have done ; but by reason of His
Saviourhood, He did not do so. For Justice' sake, and, indeed,
for man's assurance' sake, it was essential that GOD should give
some sign and indication that the One Sacrifice of our Lord was
" a full, perfect, and sufficient sacrifice, oblation and satisfaction
for the sins of the whole world ", as our Prayer Book has it. The
sign of the acceptance of the sacrifice was the resurrection, in
which, in Paul's frequent phrase, " GOD raised Him ". By that
mighty token, He is not only " declared to be the Son of GOD
with power ", as Romans i. 4 says, but also declared to be the
Saviour of men with authority. Up from the Tomb—in wondrous
resurrection ; up to the Skies—in glorious ascension ; up to
the Throne—in illustrious session. That is what GOD thinks
of the finished work of His Son. That word " highly " is the
English equivalent of a Greek preposition, " huper ", with which
the apostle has compounded the verb. Plummer points out
that Paul has a great fondness for this use. So this is a huper-
exaltation—which, greatly daring, I have elsewhere ventured
to render by the modern schoolboy slang, " Super " !

Another step up is that (ii) *God hath " given Him a Name which
is above every name* ". Here we touch upon a considerable
difference of opinion, and I must leave my readers to make up
their own minds, for there is little that is definite that I can
place before them for their guidance. (*a*) Professor Plummer, a
great Biblical expositor, seems to think that it is not an actual

4

Name that is referred to, but that it denotes the rank, or dignity, that has been given Him. "GOD gave Him the dignity that is above every dignity", as the professor put it. By the way, it is not "*a* Name", as A.V., but "*the* Name", as if that which was specially reserved for this, in recognition, and in honour, of the great task so successfully accomplished. (*b*) Bishop Lightfoot, another supreme New Testament exegete, is of a different opinion. He feels sure that an actual Name is intended ; and he points out that, in verse 10, it is not "the name JESUS", as if *it* were the Name, but "the name *of* JESUS", as if it were some other Name bestowed upon JESUS. (*c*) The more commonly held view is, of course, that this Name "JESUS" was, like the Body that bore it, raised and exalted ; and that, because of Him, it will be ever held in highest honour. This last will, in any event, always be the case ; but perhaps there was awaiting Him on His return a specially significant Name and Dignity not yet known to us. We do that sort of thing on our little sphere of earth—Sir Douglas Haig returns from a victorious campaign, and he is rewarded with a new Name and Dignity. He is to be Earl Haig. And Kitchener is to be Lord Kitchener ; and Sir John French is to be Lord French. I don't know—but these little human instances may be pale and distant illustrations of what awaited our Victorious Lord when he re-entered in triumph the Gates of Glory. Yet, be this as it may, nothing can dim for us the wonder of the sacred Name, "JESUS" : personally, I always feel that I must write it in capital letters.

> "How sweet the Name of JESUS sounds
> In a believer's ears."

So wrote a drunken sailor, John Newton, who, before his conversion, had used the Name as a swear-word.

What pages we could write on this theme ; but it is time that we set out to follow in thought His final step up into Glory. (3) "*Every tongue should confess that* JESUS CHRIST *is Lord*". "In the Name of JESUS"—not "at" (A.V.), as if every mention of it must be accompanied by a bow of the head—threefold obeisance is due, heaven and earth and under uniting to acclaim His sovereignty. Then every tongue—the atheist's tongue, the pagan's tongue, the foreign tongue, your tongue and mine—shall avow His Lordship, and our allegiance. Universal acknowledgment hereafter : how good to practise by personal confession here ! One of the most thrilling moments in the Coronation Service of our Sovereigns is that of the People's Homage, when the massed representatives of the Realm join to acclaim, "GOD

save the King ! GOD save the King ! GOD save the King ! "
But a faint echo of the great heart-moving shout of " every
tongue ". So ends our exposition of this amazing passage—
oh, that one could have done it better, more worthily. The reader
may well be constrained to throw this poor Study on one side
and to take the inspired record itself and, on his knees, pore over
the sacred words themselves ; and then, rising to his feet, join,
with deepest adoration, in the Heavenly Tribute of Revelation,
v. 12, " Worthy is the Lamb that was slain to receive power, and
riches, and wisdom, and strength, and honour, and glory, and
blessing . . . Amen ! "—One brief prosaic word must be added,
concerning—

The Way for Us

For that, after all, was how the passage began and why the
passage was penned : " Let this mind be in you, which was also
in CHRIST JESUS " (5). *The Selfless " mind "*—which thinks
nothing of itself, but only of others. *The Sacrificial " mind "*—
which is prepared to go to utmost lengths for those others'
welfare. *The Serving " mind "*—which is happily content to render
any service that will help. The late Dr. G. H. Morrison records
that he once received one of those typical postcards from Mr.
W. E. Gladstone and that it was signed as from " Your obedient
servant " ! How that would have delighted St. Paul, if II
Corinthians iv. 5 is any criterion, " We preach . . . CHRIST
JESUS the Lord, and ourselves your servant for JESUS' sake ".

VII

NOW, AND HOW

PHILIPPIANS ii. 12–13

Notice that little word " now " in verse 12, and remind yourself
that Christianity is a Religion of Now—" Behold, now is the
accepted time ; behold, now is the day of salvation ", II Corinthians vi. 2. A faith which is concerned exclusively with a past
salvation, being saved from our past sins, as it is put ; a faith
that is concerned exclusively with a future salvation, being saved
from hell's eternal penalty for our sin—both these fall short of the
New Testament conception, which visualises a present salvation ;
which tells us that we ought to enjoy, and may enjoy, a " Now "
Salvation, negatively being saved *from* the practice and habit
of daily sinning, and positively being saved *unto* the practice
and habit of daily holiness. These introductory thoughts will
serve as a useful background to the study of this interesting
and important passage, wherein Paul is pressing upon his beloved
converts a kind and quality of happy Christian life for " now ".
He starts with—

A Present Example

" Wherefore ", says the apostle—and let us remember, in all
our Bible study, how important it is to give due weight to the
conjunctions of Scripture : so much instruction is to be gleaned
from them—and here the word throws us back again to the
previous passage and bids us, as did verse 5, take note of our
Lord Jesus as our example. He " became obedient ", even
up to the extreme limit of His substitutionary death—" wherefore " we also are to be utterly obedient to God. Some of us
have yet to grasp the strategic value of this quality of plain
obedience. Trust and Obey—are the two feet on which the
Christian successfully pursues his pilgrim way ; they are the
two hands with which he grasps the great gifts of God ; they are
the two eyes to which are revealed the ever-growing truth of

GOD ; they are the two ventricles of the heart by which is shown the deep love of the Christian for his Lord.

> " Trust and Obey—for there's no other way
> To be happy in Jesus, but to trust and Obey "—

indeed, to be anything in JESUS. Not trust alone, not obedience alone ; but the two in happy partnership. Or, as the practical James would say, Faith and Works.

At this point we must recollect that when the inspired writer is urging these Philippians to take CHRIST for their example he is addressing Christians. To press upon non-Christians to follow Him thus is to mock them—such an endeavour is beyond them. They must experience Him first in another capacity. *First, as Emancipator—as Saviour.* As well tell the Hebrews to enter Canaan while they are still in Egypt as expect people to enter the Christian life when they are not yet Christians. To copy CHRIST (the secret of which we shall learn later in this very passage) is possible only to Christians. When Peter says that He has left us " an example that ye should follow His steps ", I Peter ii. 21, it is to be remembered that the " us ", and the " ye ", are believers ; and only so can they be followers. *Next, as Exemplar*—now that the order is established, the Order can be insisted upon. It is a specific command, " Be ye therefore followers of GOD, as dear children," Ephesians v. 1, the R.V. has " imitators " ; and the Greek is the word from which our " mimics " is derived. What mimics the dear children are. Some people have quarrelled with Thomas à Kempis' title " The Imitation of CHRIST ", as if that were something impossible ; but there it is, as a command of Holy Writ, and therefore possible, now that we have got things in their true sequence. *Then, as Enabler*—it is not we, but He. How often we have heard it said that GOD's commands are His enablings. If left to ourselves, it would be indeed a hopeless quest ; but we are not left like that, He is ever present with us as our daily pattern, and our constant power : His " How " for our " Now ". Some come to—

A PRESENT DUTY

" Ye have always obeyed . . . in my presence . . . now much more in my absence." Obeyed the precepts of GOD, of course, not of Paul—as CHRIST Himself, your Example, did (v. 8). Here we are, then, again at this primary Christian characteristic of obedience. And Paul felt able to bear glad acknowledgment of their upright, spiritual behaviour all the time he was with them —their daily following of the Exemplar had been exemplary. Now, however, he is far away from them, in Rome, and he is deeply concerned that their Christian consistency shall in no way be dependent upon his presence. He has said the same thing in i. 27, " Only let your [behaviour] be as it becometh the gospel of CHRIST : that whether I come . . . or else be absent, I may hear . . . that ye stand fast ". Hear, too, the apostle John, " I have no greater joy than to hear that my children walk in truth ", III John 4.

This Paul is a great student of human nature, as is evidenced in a score of passages from his pen. He knows so well how often, for moral rectitude and spiritual fidelity, we lean on one other. The convert at a mission is gloriously keen, so long as the great effort lasts, but when the evangelist is withdrawn, he begins to lose his ardour, and the Church is sad to find that he no longer walks with them. A Christian schoolboy, who had badly backslidden, said, by way of explanation, to his friend, who had left —and I heard him say it—" I was all right while you were still here ". Now, says the apostle in effect, you have been splendid in my company, " much more " let your conduct and character be true " in my absence ". But why " much more " ? Would it not have been sufficient if they had been told to continue " just the same " ? I wonder if the answer is not to be found in the fact that instead of leaning on Paul, the human prop having been removed, they are now thrown exclusively upon the Lord Himself. Many a saint could testify that they blessed GOD for some loss or trouble, because it threw them back on Him, and they came to know Him more intimately than ever they had done, or could have done before. The furnace of affliction can be a rare place for meeting and knowing GOD, as three men once discovered when they met with " the Fourth ", Daniel iii. 25. How those three would have appreciated the testimony of the Psalmist (cxix. 71), " It is good for me that I have been afflicted " ; and (verse 67) " Before I was afflicted I went astray : but now have I kept Thy word ". No wonder that, with all his experience of life, our great English poet said, " Sweet are the uses of adversity " ! The particular seeming adversity that our passage is dealing with is the removal of a trusted friend upon whom we have relied for our spiritual welfare—how " much more " blessed will that " absence " be than that " presence ", if the soul is brought to rest hard on the always-present Lord. Hebrews xiii. 5–6. Oh, that our converts—and all of us—might be encouraged to place our entire confidence thus in Him alone. So shall the life of

bedience be not only a duty, but a delight.   And now there
emerges—

A PRESENT RESPONSIBILITY

" Work out your own salvation with fear and trembling."
Some of us are so enamoured of the sheer joy of the Christian
life that we are in danger of forgetting that it is also a grave
responsibility.   It is not just a picnic !   To become a Christian
is to be invested forthwith with certain responsibilities—towards
GOD, and towards others.   It is this more serious side of our
Christianity that we are now to study, as guided by this pregnant
sentence of the apostle's.

A great Possession is conferred upon us—" your own salvation ".
(a) Of course, we must first recognise that it is His salvation
before it is yours—" Shew forth *His* salvation from day to day,"
as Psalm xcvi. 2 says, He purposed it—of His sovereign grace,
or we never would have been saved at all.   He planned it—from
before the foundation of the world, I Peter i. 20 ; the wonderful
plan was conceived in the Council Chamber of the Triune GOD.
He procured it—when the plan was put into operation at Calvary.
He proffered it—for man's acceptance, if he will have it ; for
He will not force it upon us, but will leave the gift of free-will,
with which He has endowed us, inviolate.   He pressed it—urging
man, by the continual influence of the HOLY SPIRIT, by every
means short of force, to close with the gracious offer, yet having
so often sadly to say, " How often would I . . . and ye would
not," Matthew xxiii. 37.   Ah yes, from first to last, it is His
salvation.   (b) But it became " your own " when, with the hand
of faith, you took it from the pierced hand, and what was originally
His became eternally yours.   Well, have you ?   Or are you still
without this wonderful possession ?   You could, even as you
stop a moment in reading these words, grasp the gift—yea,
grasp the Giver—now, this very minute.   And how truly wonderful the possession is—which buries the past, changes the
present, and ensures the future.   May we who have it continually
realise the wonder of this Love Gift.

A great Programme is now set before us—" work out ".   It is
sometimes held to be the teaching of this verse that we have to
work our eternal salvation out for ourselves ; but we can dismiss
this at once, because Scripture never contradicts itself, and
Ephesians ii. 9 says, it is " not of works ".   We are not to work
it into our lives, but to work it out by our lives.   Here is a great
mine.   By a catastrophic movement of nature in which the trees

were earthquaked from the surface to the depths in bygone years, GOD worked in the coal. Now it is our business to work it out for the use of man. So this mighty salvation, repository of light and warmth and energy, which is ours through the explosive dynamite (the Greek word translated " power " in Romans i. 16) of the Gospel has now to be worked out in our daily behaviour, for the blessing of our fellows and for the satisfaction of the Owner of the Mine. Thank GOD, the Christian life is a working concern : what joy, as well as responsibility, is to be found in the fact. A small boy has just gone to bed when his uncle arrives at the house, and going to his room, presents his young nephew with a lovely clockwork engine. Imagine Jack's excitement as he eagerly hopes for the morning, when he can see how it works ! Just so is it that we who have been presented with this gift— no toy—should be eager to display to others that it works. A bolder testimony, a sweeter temper, a gentler speech, a nicer manner, a keener service, a cleaner life, a kindlier behaviour, a wider helpfulness—these are some of the many ways of working it out. Reverting to our simile of the mine, I have come across this interesting sidelight. The ancient scholar Strabo (b. 64–62 B.C.), a Roman, who wrote in Greek, has an account of the once-famous silver mines in Spain, in which he refers to the " working out " of those mines, using the very same word as Paul uses here. Strabo meant, of course, as my informant proceeds, that the Romans were operating, exploiting, and getting the utmost value out of what was already securely in their possession. Such, it seems clear to me, is the apostle's meaning of " work out " —I am to mine what is already mine, producing such precious nuggets of personal character as we have just enumerated.

A great Peril is here hinted at—" with fear and trembling ". A nervous anxiety to do the right thing, thinks Lightfoot. The phrase is quite common with Paul, for instance in I Corinthians ii. 3, II Corinthians viii. 15, Ephesians vi. 5, in all which passages the meaning seems to be as the learned Bishop suggests. It is not " fear and trembling " lest we might lose our salvation, but lest we might use it amiss. It is the dread and danger of becoming so remiss in the outworking that we might cause distress to the Master, and damage to His cause. The world knows instinctively what is to be expected from the professing Christian and reserves its scorn for his failure. Think not, my friend, that, in your self-confidence, you need have no anxiety on this score. A greater than you, the apostle Peter, felt the same confidence, " I . . . never ! " Yet, how grievously he sinned. One can only say to oneself, and to others, ere we leave this subject, " Let him that thinketh he standeth, take heed lest he fall ". Oh, it is not necessary thus to falter, fail, and fall. The phrase is only intended as a warning, and as a counsel that even the most advanced Christian needs to maintain an attitude of continual watchfulness, Those who climb highest could fall farthest, if they slipped. " Hold up my goings in Thy paths, that my footsteps slip not," Psalm xvii. 5. " Unto Him that is able to keep you from falling," guard you from stumbling, Jude 24. So we come, with joyous gladness, to—

A Present Possibility

" For it is God that worketh in you both to will and to do of His good pleasure "—and that's How! First, let us look at " *His good pleasure* ". Remember how that when God had created Man and his World it is recorded that " God saw everything that He had made, and, behold, it was very good ", Genesis i. 31—very pleasing in His eyes. The glorious thing is that individual men can thus give Him joy, for of Enoch it is said that " before his translation he had this testimony, that he pleased God ", Hebrews xi. 5. Oh, to have such a testimony! In the whole body of believers, too, He is to take delight, for it is written that " Christ loved the Church, and gave Himself for it, that He might sanctify and cleanse it . . . that He might present it to Himself a glorious church, not having spot, or wrinkle, or any such thing ", Ephesians v. 25-7. And when, at the consummation, He looks out upon the whole company of the redeemed, the old prophet tells us that " He shall see of the travail of His soul, and shall be satisfied ", Isaiah liii. 11—could anything be more truly amazing : He shall feel that all His suffering for us has been worth while ? This is part of " the joy that was set before Him ", for which he was content to endure the Cross, Hebrews xii. 2. So let it be my whole, and holy, ambition—not, on any account to please myself ; nor, merely, to please others, though that is good within legitimate limits ; but always, in big things and in little things, in spiritual things and in secular things, to " please Him who hath chosen " me, II Timothy ii. 4. Now the happy present possibility that lies before each of us believers is that He is prepared, if we will let Him, so to deal with us that in our personal behaviour, and in our Christian service, and in our inner character, we shall be well-pleasing in His sight.

Look next at the all-embracing phrase, " *to will and to do* ". Here are two distinct things, psychologically apart—doing it, and desiring it. " To do "—is the problem with some of us. We need no instruction as to the right thing to do, the proper course to pursue ; it is all plain to us. But we just don't know how. One of our great scientists (I forget who it was) is reported to have said on one occasion, " If it were possible for a machine to be placed within my nature that would automatically ensure that I would always do what was right, I would close with the offer immediately ". But he knew, we know, that there is no such machine. Instead, some of us are struggling on, never expecting to do, and never succeeding in doing " His good pleasure ". " To will "—is the problem with others of us. We just don't want to : that is the plain fact ! We prefer to please ourselves ; or else, for popularity's sake, or gain's sake, we are all out to please others ; we have no real desire beyond these, no longing to please GOD. Isn't it sad ? Indeed, isn't it mad ? The late beloved F. B. Meyer relates how that once at Keswick he was confronted with some challenge of the will of GOD about which he was unwilling to surrender. On one of the surrounding hillsides the Lord wrestled with this man, as He did with Jacob, at Jabbok, long ago, Genesis xxxii. 24, until at last Meyer confessed that he was willing to be made willing ! Thus did GOD gain the victory in the life of that man that set the seal of mighty blessing upon all his subsequent ministry. If your life's problem lies here will you follow F. B. Meyer's example and let GOD know that, with all your heart, you are willing to be made willing for " His good pleasure " ?

How shall this be accomplished ? " *God that worketh in you.*" Before your conversion He worked on you, by the HOLY SPIRIT, now He works in you. Let us take note of the fact that GOD the HOLY SPIRIT is positively within every Christian. If He be not in us, we are not Christians at all, for " if any man have not the SPIRIT of CHRIST, he is none of His ", as Romans viii. 9 teaches us. Some Christians are scarcely aware of this solemn and strategic fact : consequently they are living on a low level of spiritual experience, and because they imagine that there is nothing better in store, they are content with this second-rate life—up and down ; in and out ; to and from ; on and off. It was like that with some of the Corinthian believers, just out of heathenism, and still, alas, practising some of the old uncleannesses of their former life. Says the apostle, " What ? know ye not that your body is the temple of the HOLY GHOST which is in you ? " I Corinthians vi. 19—you ought not to be unholy with the Holy One in residence ; and you need not be unholy for the indwelling Holy One is there to make you holy. He is positively within every Christian, however unsatisfactory that individual may be. He is actively within every Christian that is surrendered to Him, that lets Him work in you to bring about the doing, and the want-to. Thus are we to be " changed into the same Image . . . by the SPIRIT of the Lord ", II Corinthians iii. 18—not simply at some future date, but Now ; and this is How. Happy thought !

VIII

DARKEST PLACES NEED THE BRIGHTEST LIGHTS

PHILIPPIANS ii. 14–18

" Darkest Africa ", said H. M. Stanley long ago. " Darkest England ", said Booth more recently. Well—

Lights are made for Darkness

You may live, or work, in a dark place. A home where, sadly enough, you are the only Christian ; a workshop, factory or office where there is sheer indifference, amused contempt, or even active opposition to the things of God. You find it hard to maintain your principles, to keep up your end, to bear your witness. You know, don't you, that there is a reason for your being in such a place. God couldn't trust everybody to represent Him in such inimical circumstances—but He chose you, because He believes he can rely on you to be faithful. It is always a privilege to be trusted ; but how high an honour to be trusted by God ! " We were allowed of God to be put in trust with the gospel ", I Thessalonians ii. 4, says Paul ; and you can almost catch a tone of proper pride in his utterance. He bore, and exercised, his trust in many a difficult and dark situation, as we all know ; and so it is with you, in your trying conditions. You can't imagine a lighthouse complaining of the hardness of its lot set out there all alone on that rocky coast amid the mountainous seas and the howling tempest. If it were a sentient being, it would console itself with the reflection that that was what it was for—to hold out the light of the gospel message of comfort, safety and guidance to storm-tossed vessels battling with the hurricane and looking for the harbour. That's what you are for : if you, by God's good grace, are a light, you are just the one for a dark place. Don't disappoint His trust in you.

Take a look now at the situation of these Philippian believers, as Paul describes it. They are (i) " *In the world* " (15). It is a darksome place to live the Christian life in. At the best of times it has an unfriendly atmosphere about it ; and it is, of course, along with the flesh and the devil, one of the three sources of our temptation. In the New Testament, " the world " holds a moral significance, and, in this sense, is used to stand for all that is not of God. A worldly Christian is as a ship that has sprung a leak and allowed the sea to get in. All's well with the ship in the sea ; all's ill when the sea is in the ship. The Christian is left here " in the world ", John xvii. 11, 15 : trouble begins when he allows the world to get into him. That's how it was with one of Paul's erstwhile friends, " Demas hath forsaken me, having loved this present world ", II Timothy iv. 10. So, you see, the world is materially a location, but morally a lure.

Observe this further description of the Philippian church. (ii) " *In the midst of a crooked and perverse nation* " (15)—" genera- tion " for " nation ", please, according to both Lightfoot and Plummer. So these particular Christians were also in a dark spot. The spiritual life is not going to be easy for them either. I don't suppose your difficulties and problems are so exacting as were theirs. A " *crooked* " *people*—they were not straight, they couldn't think straight, act straight, go straight. Proverbs ii. 15, tells of people " whose ways are crooked ". The whole multitude of the Philippian neighbours was in that case—" we have turned every one to his own way ", Isaiah liii. 6, would be a perfect description of them. A " *perverse* " *people*—distorted, as the word means : they were not only out of straight, but out of shape. Like this early Christian age, how distorted are our own times—the distorted view of God, as of a placid easy-going father who will not punish sin ; the distorted view of Scripture, as of a book, very remarkable certainly, but only of human authorship and authority ; the distorted view of moral values, as of things and thoughts now out-of-date in a free, promiscuous age ; the distorted view of pleasure, as if speed, and " shows ", and silver were the prime necessities of life. " Perverse genera- tion ", says the Master, in Matthew xvii. 17 ; " speaking perverse things ", says the disciple, in Acts xx. 30. What a condition of things—men, and minds, and moments of darkness : just what lights are made and meant for !

LIGHTS ARE SUBJECT TO INFLUENCE

There are things that help, and things that hinder. Of course, if we are not " sons of God " (15), there is no light at all in our souls, and we cannot be as lights to others. Unless, and until, we have entered into the family of God we have not really begun

to live in the Scriptural and eternal sense, whatever our other
accomplishments may be. That was what astonished Nicodemus
at his night interview with JESUS. This highly educated, civil
and ecclesiastical leader, and good-living man, come to discuss
the new doctrine of this New Teacher, is suddenly held up, at
the outset of the conversation, and challenged with the devastating
statement that he had not yet begun—" Ye must be born again ",
John iii. 7. It seems that he did thus begin that night—judging
from his shy remark in vii. 50, and his open action in xix. 30.
Have you begun ?

Well now, on *the Hindering side*—" murmurings and disputings " (14) : the inward and the outward respectively, the
veiled and the open, probably in relation to GOD ; " the moral
and the intellectual rebellion against GOD " says Lightfoot.
There is doubtless a reference here to the murmurings of the
children of Israel, Numbers xx. 2 ; xxi. 5. " Neither murmur ye,
as some of them murmured ", I Corinthians x. 10. There can be
no red light unless there is perfect alignment and adjustment
with Him. Do you think there is some hint of this in the Master's
saying in John viii. 12—" I am the Light of the World, he that
followeth Me shall not walk in darkness, but shall have the light
of life ". Let me suggest an allusion. On a clear night, you look
up into the sky and say to your friend, " How brightly the moon
is shining ". You should say, of course, " How brightly the sun
is shining ", for the moon has no light of her own. She is only
reflecting the light of the sun. You can't see it, for the sun has
long since " gone down " ; but the moon keeps her face to that
light, and so walks in the light. If she were, by a fraction, to
turn her face away—any " murmurings and disputings "—there
would be no light. Transfer all this to our Lord's words. He
is that Sun—" the Sun of Righteousness ", Malachi iv. 2 ; we
are that Moon, a luminary in the dark place ; as we " follow "
in the Sun's track and orbit, with undeviating obedience, " without murmurings and disputings ", we catch the Light and
convey it to a darkling world. Thus " we all with open [unveiled]
face beholding . . . the glory of the Lord, are changed into the
same image from glory to glory ", II Corinthians iii. 18—only
let all the glory be ascribed, not to us, but to Him : not " How
bright the Moon is, but " How bright the Sun is " ! Very well
then, " no disputings "—no cross-purposes.

And next, on *the Helping side*—" blameless, and harmless,
without rebuke " (15). Plummer suggests that these three negative adjectives should be understood to mean—free from blame,
free from adulteration, free from blemish. The lights of Paul's

day would be derived from oiled wicks ; and if you are old enough to have had experience of oil lamps, you will remember how the light was dimmed and impeded by those excrescenses that sometimes adhered to the wick—and how the light leaped to its proper brightness when the wick was trimmed. To be free of all adhesions of the evil is such a help towards the bright light of Christian testimony. Do you remember that wonderful picture of the living Lord " in the midst of the seven candlesticks ", Revelation i. 13—that is, the seven churches, most of whose wicks are seen, in chapters ii. and iii., to be cluttered with moral and spiritual accretions, dimming their light. So we observe this " One like unto " the Son of Man " trimming the lamps. That same Lord JESUS would so readily trim our light, too, if we gave Him the chance. What a help that would be —no impediments. We have heard talk of spots on the sun : let there be no spots on you !

LIGHTS ARE BEARERS OF BLESSING

Where there are no lights there are always possible dangers, and often there is sin. Recall that startling disclosure of certain evil hearts, in John iii. 19, " This is the condemnation, that Light is come into the world, and men loved darkness rather than light, because their deeds were evil ". Think of that horse-riding messenger traversing an unfamiliar coast road with a most important communication, at dead of night, who, in a sudden flash of lightning, finds that he is on the very edge of a precipitous cliff—what a blessing was that brilliant light. Think of that lonely, wounded soldier, returning to consciousness, miserably lost, out on the South African veldt : he has a compass in his pocket, but it is useless, because he can't see it in the black darkness ; then he observes a tiny light seemingly approaching him ; yes, it is a wee glow-worm, by whose light he is just able to read his compass and eventually to find his way to the English lines—what a blessing was that little light. You and I, my reader, whether great or little lights, what a help we might be " in the world ", if only we would shine—aiding some to see, and escape, the dangerous precipice of sin, aiding others wounded and lost in sin to find their way home to GOD. Oh, the joy of being a light like this. Our Lord said, " I am the light of the World ", John viii. 12, as we saw just now. He also said, " Ye are the light of the world ", Matthew v. 14. What a privilege ! It is His light that we get into ourselves, and then give out to others. It isn't always easy ; but what a happiness !

Our passage describes it as " Holding forth the word of life "
(16)—which changes the metaphor, but not the meaning.
" Holding forth " should be " holding out ", as if offering a
gift. What an offer is this that we are entrusted with ; what a
responsibility is thereby ours ; what a mixed reception it will
meet with ; what a variety of ways in which it can be proffered.
This " word of life " is but another name for the light ; for remember Psalm cxix. 105, " Thy word is a lamp unto my feet,
and a light unto my path ". On a certain ocean liner, a passenger
was lying in his cabin seriously ill. One dark night he heard a
cry " Man overboard ", and while sensitive to all the excitement
and hurry, he was too unwell to give any help. One of the difficulties was that they could not see the man. All of a sudden,
however, a light shone out through the glass of a port-hole. It
happened to fall full on the struggling man in the water, so that
they were able to throw him a life-belt and then go to his rescue.
Whence came that light ? From the sick man, who, feeling so
distressed at his incapacity to help, managed to crawl out of
his bunk, take the lantern down from the wall, and place it
where it could shine forth. Imagine his joy when he learned that
it was he and his lantern that had saved the man. What a light
was that man, what a light was that lantern. If we would be
lights shining for souls drowning, not in the sea, but in sin, we
shall do it best by knowing, by using, and by living the lantern of
God's word.

LIGHTS HAVE FIRST TO BE LIT

This is, I think, what lies behind the rest of our verse 16—that
Paul looks forward to rejoicing at the judgment seat of CHRIST,
when the Christian's work shall be estimated, I Corinthians iii. 13,
that his own work shall prove to have been not as a lost race, nor
as lost labour, that it shall appear that he had been GOD's light
to light these Philippian lights that were to " shine as lights in
the world ". Paul had set them alight. That is generally GOD's
way : nearly always He uses human instruments. And sometimes it is lesser lights that light larger lights—matches ignite
torches. What a torch Peter was : it was the smaller Andrew
that set a match to him. John i. 42. What a torch Nehemiah
became : it was the almost unknown Hanani that set him aflame,
Nehemiah i. 2. Have you heard of that torch, C. H. Spurgeon ?
Yes, but have you known the name of the match, that old lay
preacher that winter's morning in the Colchester chapel? Have
you ever heard of a Mr. Kemball ? You should have, for his

name is well known in heaven—he was only a match, but he set a great torch alight, Dwight L. Moody. You will have heard of Maria Millis ? No ? Well, have you heard of the Earl of Shaftesbury ? Yes, of course—he was the torch, but she was the match : his childhood nurse, who sowed the seed, struck the spark, lit the flame. We can't all be torches, but we can all be matches—though we ourselves are of such insignificant personality as a match, we can, if we are lit, set another ablaze for GOD as a veritable torch. Ah, and more than one. Have you ever played that parlour game, How many candles can you light with one match ?

This was the employ that gave Paul the greatest joy of his life —to have led Timothy into the light, " my own son in the faith ", I Timothy i. 2 ; or Titus, " mine own son after the common faith ", Titus i. 4 ; or Onesimus, " whom I have begotten in my bonds ", Philemon 10 ; or Philemon himself, " thou owest unto me even thine own self ", Philemon 19 ; and many, many another, including the recipients of this Epistle, " my joy and crown ", Philippians iv. 1. Make it your aim, my reader, to light as many candles as you can with your match, even if you suffer the burning of your own fingers. You were not lit for yourself alone.

> Have you had a kindness [" the kindness ", Titus iii. 4] shewn ?
>> Pass it on !
> 'Twas not meant for thee alone,
>> Pass it on !
> Let it travel down the years,
> Let it dry another's tears,
> Till in heaven the deed appears,
>> Pass it on !

Doggerel, did you say ? Well, good sense, anyway—and even, spiritually, good manners. Paul has in mind the idea of that last longer line, " till in heaven the deed appears ", when he speaks of his desire to " rejoice in the day of CHRIST ". May we, too, have that joy. The late Dean Vaughan, bygone famous trainer of aspiring young ministers of the Gospel—who, by the way, were dubbed " Vaughan's doves " used, in his last lecture to them, to say, " Gentlemen, whatever else you are or do, make sure that you so order your life and ministry that when you get up yonder there shall be many a one who shall take you by the hand and lead you to the Throne and say, ' Lord, in Thy power, this man brought me here ' ". Yes, indeed, bliss for the soul-winner, the life-lighter, Here and Hereafter. But—

5

Lights are Sacrificial Things

Do you recall how that, when referring to that flaming torch, John Baptist, our Lord said, " He was a burning and a shining light ", John v. 35—there is no shining without burning. The rule is clearly evident in the disappearing wax of the candle, or in the consumption of the oil of the lamp ; but it is true in all cases, there is no light without combustion. So the remainder of this present passage is concerned with the sacrificial aspect of the Christian life.

The allusion of verse 17 is to a practice operating in both Jewish and heathen religions. We may assume that it was the latter that Paul referred to, inasmuch as the Philippian Christians would scarcely be familiar with Jewish ways ; but, having themselves just come out from heathendom, they would at once catch the allusion to the pagan rites. When certain annual sacrifices were made, the custom was to accompany the offering with a pouring of wine. Joseph tells us that in Jewish sacrifices this drink offering, ᴐᴛᴀᴍᴀᴋᴀᴠᴀ ᴀᴠᴛ ᴊⱼ ᴡᴀᴀ ᴘᴏᴜᴇᴅ " ᴀᴛᴏᴜᴎᴅ " the altar ; whereas in the heathen rite, the libation was poured " *upon* " the victim. It is " upon " that is used here, which I take to strengthen the suggestion that the apostle's reference is to the heathen practice. This being clear, we may now conclude that Paul thinks of their sacrifice as the Oblation and his blood-shedding, when it comes, as the Libation. Listen to Lightfoot's summing-up, " The Philippians are the priests ; their faith (or their good works springing from their faith) is the sacrifice ; Paul's life-blood the accompanying libation ". In this mutual self-giving, the apostle finds cause for mutual gladness—" I joy, and rejoice " (17) ; " ye joy, and rejoice " (18).

Darkest places need the brightest lights. How true ! Let us see to it that by God's grace there shall be no damage to our testimony, that might cause shipwreck, alas, to any soul. May I repeat W. Y. Fullerton's great story ? One night, off the Florida coast, a tempestuous gale was blowing. The violence of the wind was so terrific that it stove in the glass of one of the sides of the lantern of the lighthouse set to guard that part of the treacherously rocky shore. The keeper had no other glass to cover the gap and shield the lamp, and doing his best, he fixed in a sheet of tin. In the storm a harassed ship was beating up, trying to find harbour, and not finding a light that he knew should be there the captain got confused and ran his vessel on to the rocks, when boat and all hands were lost. Why ? Because the light-house had one part dark ! I go straight to Luke xi. 36, " having no part dark "—oh, the damage, even the shipwreck, we may cause to another soul and life, if by some unjudged habit, some wretched inconsistency, some slack behaviour, some " part dark ", obscuring the light, we bring loss to others.   Let us close our meditation with the prayer that we may be " full of light ", and full of the " joy " of our concluding verses.

IX

A COUPLE OF FINE SPECIMENS

PHILIPPIANS ii. 19-30

WE have just been thinking about lights, and here now we have two magnificent examples. Two Christian men utterly consistent, good, through and through. It used to be said that the difference between linoleum and cork-linoleum was that in the one the pattern was on top and eventually wore off, but in the other the pattern went right through. This was the style of these two men —Christian all through, inward and outward. The late beloved Bishop Taylor Smith used to say, " It isn't the label on the bottle, but what's inside ". With Epaphroditus and Timothy the two coincided—Christian in name, Christian in nature.

The passage is a homely one and reflects the real affection existing, on both sides, between Paul and his beloved Philippians. Let us get the picture clear. Back in the summer these European Christians had sent Epaphroditus to Rome to carry a gift to Paul in prison. Now, according to Professor David Smith, it is November, and Paul has not yet acknowledged the present— not that he was unappreciative of their kindness, nor that he was careless of such a courtesy, but just that he had had no one to send. You couldn't, in those days, pop a letter in a pillar-box ! Meanwhile, Epaphroditus had been given instructions by the Philippian church that he was, having delivered the goods, to stay by the apostle for a while and help him in any way he could. This he did to such purpose that he made himself ill—so ill, that he was like to die. However, to Paul's relief and joy, he was spared and raised up to life and service again. His distress now was that the Philippian friends, who had sent him, had got wind of his illness and were worrying about how things were going with him, and was he getting on ? Paul, therefore, unselfish as ever, decides to send him back to his own people—he will, in that case, be able to carry the apostle's belated thanks for their generosity to him, and they will also have the comfort and satisfaction of getting their friend home once more. For his own part, Paul expects to be able to visit Philippi at some future date. At the moment that cannot be, for he is a prisoner and must await his appearance in court; but as soon as he knows how his case has gone, he will be off to see them [which, probably he did]. Before he can himself get started, he will send their highly esteemed friend, Timothy, to bring them the news of the decision—for there was no wireless then. And, as they await the result, Epaphroditus is dispatched, carrying with him this priceless letter, so full of affectionate happiness. There is the story; and now let us examine the verses, in more particular reference to these two typical specimens of the all-out and all-round Christian.

READY TO GO ANYWHERE

Suppose GOD planned to send you to some dark pagan corner of the globe to be His light to benighted, groping, heathen souls, would you go? Said Henry Martin, on the eve of his departure for the dark mission-field, " I go to burn out for GOD ". Would you be prepared for that, if it proved to be GOD's will for you? Here before us are two men ready, any moment, to go anywhere on Paul's errands in the service of the Master. Note Paul's decision " to send Timotheus " (19), and " to send Epaphroditus " (25). He knew there was no question of their prompt obedience, nor of their consulting their own convenience.

How interesting it is to mark this fine quality in GOD's servants to go wherever they be sent, in spite of the errand being fraught with possible danger. Look at some. " *And Moses went*," Exodus iv. 18—yes, back to Egypt, from which, forty years before, he had fled for his life. He had made every excuse for not going; but, when he saw that this was GOD's plan for him, he " went ". And to what purpose. " *And Elijah went*," I Kings xviii. 2—sent to go and meet cruel undisciplined Ahab, who had been searching the land to find him that he might silence his awkward, prophetic ministry. In this case it seems that there was no hesitation. As soon as GOD's plan was plain, he " went ", to what a scene of triumph for JEHOVAH on Carmel. " *And Philip went*," Acts viii. 27—but he was the leader of a great revival movement in Samaria. Surely, it must be a mistake; it would appear to be clear that he cannot be spared from his truly strategic position as centre, and pivot, of the widespread blessing. Especially as he is bidden to betake himself to a desert region and eventually to devote himself to one man. Spite of what must have been his mystification, he " went "—to lead that one highly placed official to CHRIST, and who, in his turn, was seemingly used to the founding of the once-virile church in

North Africa. What a good thing he went! "*And Ananias went,*" Acts ix. 17—it was surely putting his head in the lion's mouth. This Saul of Tarsus, arch-persecutor, and here in Damascus for that very intent—again, there must be some mistake. When, however, this disciple was reassured, he "went", and had the joy of being the first Christian to give to this remarkable convert the right hand of fellowship, and the first to minister to his deep need. Thanks be to GOD for these, and others, who so bravely "went" on GOD's errands. I remember hearing the saintly F. B. Meyer, then still preaching at eighty-two, say "I have only one ambition: to be GOD's errand-boy"! How beautifully in tune with that lovely self-portrait of Gabriel, which I love to quote, in Luke i. 19, "I am Gabriel that stand in the presence of GOD, and am sent . . ." That was the intention of the Master for His disciples, "He ordained twelve, that they should be with Him, and that He might send them. . . ." Mark iii. 14. Might He have us, to be absolutely at His disposal, to take messages anywhere?

READY TO HELP ANYONE

Note this spirit of helpfulness in the case of Timothy (20-1). Here are what one might call three directions of help. (*a*) *Ourselves*—"all seek their own". How common a trait it is, in the generality of people, to be always careful to look after Number One. Even when such folk do good things, it is only to gain kudos and a reputation for themselves: they are of the same ilk as the "hypocrites" of Matthew vi. 2 f, who performed the creditable functions of giving, praying and fasting; "to be seen of men", "that they may have glory of men". I—is their god; Self—is their goal; Me, Me, Me—is their slogan. Well now, Timothy was not one of these, as the implication of the passage shews. (*b*) *Others*—"who will naturally care for your state" (20). That was this young man's outlook. When Sir Bartle Frere returned from India the carriage was sent to the village station to bring him to his home. When the new footman, but newly engaged, asked how he should recognise Sir Bartle, his aged mother said, "Look out for somebody helping someone else". Sure enough, when the London train had drawn in, the manservant observed a gentleman assisting an old lady to the platform and then jumping back into the carriage to fetch out her luggage. Going straight up to him, the footman enquired, "Sir Bartle?" Yes; it was he. What a lovely reputation to have! To be known as one who is always on the look-out to see when, and how, one can help others. Others: yes, that was a supreme characteristic of the Master, "He saved others," Matthew xxvii. 42. I suspect it was a mark of Timothy's life also. Do you observe that word "naturally" in verse 20? He was a Christian, and was therefore a possessor of that new nature that comes from the indwelling of the HOLY SPIRIT. It should always be a quite natural thing for a Christian man to be an "others" man, for "the fruit of the SPIRIT is love", Galatians v. 22. Non-Christian people sometimes display this quality of others-ness. With them, it is like apples tied on a tree; with us it is fruit growing out naturally. But, but, but —is it always so seen in us Christians? Are not we sometimes very self-centred, self-seeking, shewing little of the "care" of others which was so manifest a feature in Timothy's make-up? Described as we are, in Isaiah lxi. 3, as "trees of righteousness, the planting of the Lord, that He might be glorified", we have become fruitless trees, and He is not glorified, and others have not been helped. (c) Our Lord—"the things which are JESUS CHRIST'S" (21). The inference here is that those who help others help Him. We know how the opposite of that is true, for we remember how the Living Lord says to Saul, "Why persecutest thou Me?" It was the Christians he was hurting. Yes; and, in so doing, he was hurting Him. We recall, too, His words, "Inasmuch as ye have done it . . . done it unto Me. Inasmuch as ye did it not . . . did it not to Me," Matthew xxv. 40, 45. All this apart, there are those, and Timothy was one of them, whose lives are devoted, not consciously to their own interests, but to the concerns of the Lord—who care, above all else, that His Name shall be honoured among men, that His Kingdom shall be furthered through the world, that His Will shall be done in earth as it is done in heaven, Matthew vi. 9-10. Here, then, is Timothy, ready to help anyone, whether in secular, or whether in spiritual matters; anxious above all to help his spiritual "father" (22). Many a little fellow loves to help daddy; many a grown-up son counts it a joy and privilege to help the old gentleman. Just so was Timothy—as the Philippians had "proved" (22)—eager to serve with Paul in the fellowship, and adventure, of "the gospel". Only let Paul use him to the full, and the young protégé was happy, whatever be the difficulties that were in the way. Paul, on his part, is so glad to use so enthusiastic a helper, and sends him hither and thither on gospel errands—to Philippi, almost immediately (23), to Ephesus to take up the oversight of the churches in the vicinity (I Timothy

i. 3). The man will prove a succourer of many—of any he can help.

Note this spirit of helpfulness also in the case of Epaphroditus (25–30). Paul writes of him as " he that ministered to my wants ". For " ministered " he uses an interesting word. He could have employed other words, but he chooses this which, as a matter of fact, refers specifically to Temple service—as if the things this man did for the apostle were of a religious nature, because done also for the Lord. Verily, there is nothing secular that is done for JESUS' sake—even " a cup of cold water ". Never forget that when this same apostle writes, in I Corinthians xii. 28 about great spiritual gifts, " first apostles, secondarily prophets, thirdly teachers, after that miracles, then gifts of healings . . . governments, diversities of tongues," he has in that blank space the word " helps ". Those other things are out of the reach of most of us, but we can all be helps. What a help Epaphroditus was " My brother "—fellow-believers : as such born into the family of the Father, All His sons are brothers of each other. Alas, we don't always behave brotherly towards our fellow-Christians, as Galatians vi. 10 says we ought " especially " to do. My " companion in labour "—fellow-worker : no distinction drawn between the foreman and the ordinary hand. The apostle places his helper as on the same footing in this building operation. My " fellow-soldier "—fellow-campaigner in this " World War One " against all the allied forces of entrenched evil. Then Paul turns to simpler tasks performed by this helper. " Your messenger "—the one sent by the Philippian church with the love and largesse of the believers there. He had doubtless, with gladness, accepted this commission. Lastly, " that ministered to my wants "—what were these wants, and how catered for, we do not know. What we do know is that he wore himself out in this " Temple ministry ". As the passage ends, " to supply your lack of service toward me "—it doesn't mean that they were ignorant of his need, nor idle to supply it, but that, for some while, they had had no chance to do what their heart longed to do. All that distance over land and sea away, they had no one to take the supplies, until Epaphroditus had become available for the purpose. And now, Paul reports, his friend " was full of heaviness "—full of gladness that he was the better of his sickness, but so sorry because the news of his grave illness had somehow reached Philippi, and he knew how grieved and anxious they would be. Thus is revealed the deep affection of all to each. How Paul loved Timothy and Epaphroditus ; how they loved him. How Paul loved the Philippians ; how they

loved him.   How Epaphroditus (and even Timothy, 20) loved the
Philippians ; how they loved him.   See how these Christians
loved one another !

Ere we come to consider a last thought or two from our passage,
may we turn aside to ponder the sad lack of love in the Church
to-day.   There is no lack of learning—and we welcome it all,
as it seeks to unravel for us the secrets of GOD's universe and
GOD's truth.   There is no lack of organisation—and we recognise
the usefulness of it, so long as it does not strangle the organism.
There is no lack of busy-ness—alas, that so much of it is not real
business.   There is, however, a strange and sad lack of love—
and love is the true test of discipleship.   Are you a Christian ?
Here is the sign by which you may be sure : listen carefully :
" We know that we have passed from death unto life, because
we love. . . ." I John iii. 14.   Do others know we are Christians ?
Here is the test : listen carefully : " By this shall all men know
that ye are My disciples, if ye have love. . . ." John xiii. 35.
Oh, that all we Christians everywhere would pray, and pray
again, and yet again for a great baptism of love, as in the first
days of the Church.   What revolutions would be brought to pass.
We cannot achieve this by any energy of our own : the secret
lies in the full understanding and experience of Romans v. 5.
And now back to our passage, where we shall find our two good
specimens—

READY TO SACRIFICE ANYTHING

We thought in our last Study of the self-sacrifice involved
in the light.   A single phrase written in the account of these
two men will be sufficient to indicate the same truth in their
case, magnificent lights that they are.   (i) " *Served with me in the
Gospel* " (22).   A fellow-slave, for so strong is the word.   It is
interesting to observe how anxious Paul seems to have been
to hold both these men as equal partners with himself in the
pursuit of the great advantage.   By the way, the word " in "
here should be " unto ", unto the Gospel : Plummer translates
it " for the promotion of "—you get the same thing in i. 5.
Here, then, is Timothy slaving away, alongside his father in
GOD, sharing the hardships, the perils, the chances of the campaign.   All which conjures up in our minds a young man of tough
constitution—yet, how different is the case.   Look at him as
he really is, as the records describe him.   (*a*) *His sheltered home*—
" I call to remembrance the unfeigned faith that is in thee,
which dwelt first in thy grandmother Lois, and thy mother

Eunice ", II Timothy i. 5. Picture of a quiet and godly home, with Tiny Tim reared in the Scriptures (II Timothy iii. 15) and brought up in the faith of GOD, which afterwards, when a boy of say, fifteen, grew into the Christian belief. (b) *His delicate health*—" Use a little wine for thy stomach's sake and thine often infirmities ", I Timothy v. 23. Mark that he says " a little " ! (c) *His sensitive nature*—" let no man despise thy youth ", I Timothy iv. 12. So does Paul feel it necessary to take the stand compatible with his position of the Oversight of the Ephesian churches ; he is not to be upset by the possible attitude of supercilious superiority of some who might reflect upon the fewness of his years, and the narrowness of his experience. What impression, I wonder, was made upon this shy, timid soul by the news—and possibly even the sight—of the stoning of Paul in his native Lystra, Acts xiv. 19. It was there and then, it seems, that Timothy became a believer in that faith for which Paul suffered, and in which he continued to grow, being " well reported of " by the Christians there. And when Paul was next in Lystra, amongst other things looking for another young fellow to join his mission party in place of the deserted Mark, it was to this convert of his that he turned, and constrained to throw in his lot with him, Acts xvi. i. 1–3. So it came to pass that this so unlikely person, knowing full well what of privation, danger, and suffering it might mean, as Paul had already undergone, yet ventured forth with him, utterly regardless of his own comfort and feelings. Tradition has it that he was ultimately clubbed to death, after a life of toil and tumult. Ready for anything was this heroic young man, with self always sacrificed to CHRIST and His cause. Can the Master count upon us for a like complete surrender of ourselves " for the promotion of the Gospel " ?

We turn, in conclusion, to that second man, and note, in the account of him, this illuminating phrase, " not regarding his life " (30). The Greek word of seventeen letters translated " not regarding " is a picturesque one, and really signifies " hazarding ", or gambling. We naturally think of Paul and Barnabas, who, in Acts xv. 26, are described, though there a different word is used, as " men that have hazarded their lives for the Name of our Lord JESUS CHRIST ". Epaphroditus belonged to that same fine company ; " indeed he was sick night unto death " (27). We may presume that he was a well-enough man when he left Philippi, and that he contracted no trouble on the journey, but that he took the deadly disease owing to his unflagging, self-forgetful zeal for Paul's service, and the work of GOD, in Rome. Do you remember that the runaway thief, the slave Onesimus, was found in the slums of Rome—" the common sink of all the worst vices of humanity ", as Lightfoot called it—and brought to Paul in his prison, where he was converted, Philemon 10 ? I wonder who discovered him, and fetched him ? Was this the kind of thing that Epaphroditus was doing ? Was it there, in the fœtid atmosphere of the squalid environs of the back streets and hiding-places of Imperial Rome, that he caught his germ ? Run down with strenuous labour, he might so easily have become susceptible to some venomous virus. So, in very zeal he gambled with his life " for the work of CHRIST " (30). The late Professor Deissman, in his *Light from the Ancient East*, has told us that at Alexandria there was a large guild (and it seems that there were similar brotherhoods elsewhere), called the Parabolani (a name akin to this word for " hazarding "), who risked their lives in visiting the sick and burying the dead during the plague. In the early church there were those who missed the martyr's death, but deserved the martyr's crown.

Yes, here were two valiants, Ready for Anything. How much does GOD see us ready for ? How fine a slogan it would be for all of us Christians, who are enlisted as good soldiers of JESUS CHRIST, II Timothy ii. 3, just four vows—Anywhere ! Anyone ! Anything ! Any cost !

X

PROFIT AND LOSS ACCOUNT

PHILIPPIANS iii. 1–11

BEFORE taking up the main theme, let us deal with one or two other matters that are mentioned at the opening of the passage. " *Finally, my brethren* "—as if he is thinking of concluding the letter ; we have the same thing at iv. 8. In both cases, how glad we are that the Epistle did not end there—for there follow, in each instance, precious utterances that we should be sorry indeed to miss. " *Rejoice in the Lord* " —everything for Paul is " in the Lord " : it is, as Plummer says, the Christian's natural environment. " *To write the same things to you* "—reiteration is one of the great rules of a good teacher, and the apostle was one of the best of tutors. For instance, this " Rejoice " of his, how often he repeats it—yet never so often as to be " grievous ", or irksome, to himself, nor unnecessary to their welfare. The reiterations of GOD make a moving study " The word of the Lord came unto Jonah the second time ", Jonah iii. 1 ; " GOD hath spoken once ; twice have I heard this, that power belongeth unto GOD ", Psalm lxii. 11 ; " How often would I . . . . and ye would not ", Matthew xxiii. 37 ; " Behold I [keep on standing, Gk.] at the door, and I [keep on knocking] . . .", Revelation iii. 20. Our Lord Himself did the same thing ; and often when there seem to be discrepances as between the two utterances of what appears to be the identical statement, there turns out to be no contradiction, but He is repeating a story, an illustration, in different contexts, and He alters the form somewhat to suit other circumstances, other audiences. Have you noticed that, while in Luke xv. 4, He tells about the Lost Sheep in allusion to the publicans, He repeats the story, in Matthew xviii. 12, in relation to the children ? All we preachers occasionally repeat an old sermon ! Ah yes, there is value in reiteration. " *Beware of* [*the*] *dogs, beware of* [*the*] *evil workers, beware of* [*the*] *concision* "—the presence, in the Greek, of the definite article shows that he is referring, not to these dangers in general, as A.V. might suggest, but to particular people, whose activities were well known to the readers. Wherever Paul worked he was, it seems, opposed by, troubled by, one or other of two powerful false teachings—Judaism, or Gnosticism. In Colossians, it was particularly the latter that was the problem ; in Philippians, it was the former, with their strong and specific demand that all Christians must adhere to the Mosaic law, and be circumcised. By this and other aberrations from the truth, these people [like some 'Isms, and 'Ists of to-day] were a constant menace and nuisance. " Dogs " —Paul calls them, for he can be very blunt in his language. He does not mean the little pet dogs of the home that JESUS mentions in Matthew xv. 26, but the Eastern ill-conditioned, pariah dogs that prowl for garbage, whose bark was unnerving, and whose bite was poisonous. Jews always called Gentiles " dogs "—as Paul himself would have done in his unconverted days ; but now he turns the opprobrious epithet upon these Judaisers. " Evil workers "—they certainly are, sowing the seeds of doubt, sapping the strength of confidence and enthusiasm, stopping the testimony of some who were once so keen. " The concision "—Paul labels them, which means a " cutting ". Circumcision was a sacred rite ; but these people had robbed it of all truly religious significance, and made it no more than a physical formality—it was as worthless as the gashings of the prophets of Baal, in I Kings xviii. 25. " *We are the circumcision* "—the true circumcision, the inheritors of that for which the old covenant rite stood. " Know ye therefore that they which are of faith, the same are the children of Abraham ", Galatians iii. 7. " We worship GOD ", not merely in the letter, but " in the spirit " ; and we " rejoice " in having the One for whom the old covenant was the preparation ; and we set no store by the mere cutting of " the flesh ". In the words of our Church of England Collect, we look for " the true circumcision of the spirit ". There we may finish our preliminary considerations, and go on now to the main teaching of the passage. The apostle is very quick to seize upon anything in common life to provide him with an illustration of spiritual truth. How apt was his Master in that same practice. So now the apostle goes to the world of business and brings out a meditation on spiritual accountancy, drawing up for himself, and for our instruction, what we have called a " Profit and Loss Account ". He says " I counted " (7), " I count " (8), " I count " (8).

THE PROFITS THAT PROVED LOSS

What a list of investments he puts down. Gilt-edged securities, he had considered them, but they had grossly depreciated, and

now he was forced to write them off as worth just nothing. The
scrip was just scrap. Let us look them over for our guidance
in our Life's business. (1) "*Circumcised the eighth day*"—which
shows that he was a true Jew; Ishmaelites were circumcised
at thirteen years old; proselytes—that is, Gentiles who embraced
the Jewish faith—were circumcised at any age, upon admission
to Judaism. Paul never forgot his Jewish nationality, and
wherever he went he always sought to preach first in the syna-
gogue. Only after they refused him a hearing did he assert,
"Your blood be upon your own heads; I am clean; from
henceforth I will go unto the Gentiles ", Acts xviii. 6. Though
he became the apostle of the Gentiles, and though he is writing
to Gentiles, he yet says, "To the Jew first ", Romans i. 16;
and in the very same Epistle (x. 1), he declares, "My heart's
desire and prayer to God for Israel is, that they might be saved ".
Are we so earnest for the spiritual blessing and welfare of the
nation to which we belong ? (2) "*Of the stock of Israel*"—this
is the religious name of the nation, and meant so much to the
real, pious Jew. Paul would assess the material value of the
ancient people as very high, but it was, for him, the spiritual
side that held highest honour. To have come from such a stock
was privilege indeed. (3) "*Of the tribe of Benjamin*"—what a
tribe to belong to. "Little Benjamin ", as the Psalmist affection-
ately called it, Psalm lxviii. 27. It was specially noteworthy
for its having the Holy City within its borders, and as being the
birthplace of the people's first king, after whom Paul's Jewish
name was taken. Inhabitants thereof are proud of being
Lancastrians, Devonians, Northumbrians, and so on: thus
would some Israelites be proud of being a Benjaminian, or is it
Benjamite ? Paul was. (4) "*An Hebrew of the Hebrews*"—
though living at Tarsus, Acts xi. 25, and educated at the great
University there, Paul was pure Jew. Concerning Timothy it
is said, Acts xvi. 1, that "his father was a Greek "; but there
was no such heathen blood in our apostle. Both his parents were
pure Jews, so that he is properly here described as "a Hebrew
sprung from Hebrews ". One can imagine how, as a rising young
Rabbi in training, he set so much value on his pure, unmixed
descent. He felt that, in his future work, it would stand him in
good stead. (5) "*As touching the law, a Pharisee*"—this was
his religious adherence, and he would be very strict in all the
daily observance of "the law ", with all the Scribal accretions
attached; he would be very haughty in demeanour. As a sect,
they came under the scathing denunciation of our Lord, because
of the arrogance of their outward conduct alongside the putridity

of their inward corruption—"whited sepulchres", as He called them, Matthew xxiii. 27. There was, of course, a different type of Pharisee, strongly political, eager nationalist, anti-Roman, who, especially during their history in the time between the Old and New Testaments, the period of the Maccabees, showed heroic qualities on behalf of their race. Ah well, they were a mixed company ; but we have a feeling that Paul himself was of the ardent, the upright, the better sort. (6) " *Concerning zeal, persecuting the church* "—how praiseworthy and creditable it had seemed. As an abnormally young member of the Sanhedrin, he had, from the first, been in touch with what he would then deem the heretical JESUS movement. He may even have been present at the Trial ; but now He was dead and done for—making Himself equal with GOD, indeed ! But this man, in his fanatical indignation, was not going to sit at ease ; he would stamp out the remembrance of the Nazarene's name, and root out every disciple and believer. So it was that " Saul . . . made havoc of the church ", Acts viii. 3. Until the dramatic moment when he heard the dead Man's voice again—amazed, arrested, " apprehended " (12). How gloriously he brought all his gifts, and all his zeal, into the service of his new-found Master and Saviour. (7) " *Touching the righteousness which is in the law, blameless* "—One thinks at once of that other religious young man, who, under the gaze of holy, penetrating eyes, was able to say of the law's demands, " Master, all these have I observed from my youth ", Mark x. 20. Concerning Saul, as he then was, Plummer writes, " Minute duties were scrupulously performed, and no Pharisee, however strict, could have blamed him for laxity ". Would that we were as " blameless " relating to the Christian code.

There it all is, then—what riches they once had seemed ; but now it had all fallen about his ears. It took his blinded eyes to see how worthless it all was. His spiritual finance was in a hopeless tangle. Becoming his own auditor, he could only certify the whole as dead loss, and himself a miserable and hopeless bankrupt. " What things were gain to me, those I counted loss. . . ." (7). It is time we went into the other side of his Account.

THE LOSSES THAT PROVED PROFIT

There was a queer transposition of the credit and debit sides of the account. Look at it. " I have suffered the loss of all things " (8). *He had lost financial stability*—at one time he had

doubtless lived an affluent life ; he could not have studied at
Tarsus University, nor moved later in Pharisaical and Sanhedrin
circles unless he and his family were quite well-to-do. Now he
was a poor man, often, for his livelihood, depending upon his
craft of tent-making, Acts xviii. 3, and sometimes reduced to
accepting gifts from his friends for his provision, iv. 11–12.
He had lost physical comfort—it would appear that, from the
time of his conversion, he was cut off from his family, for they
are never mentioned, and he was condemned to a life of privation
and suffering such as has fallen to the lot of few. Read his own
account of it, in II Corinthians xi. 23–8—" labours, stripes,
prisons, rods, stoned, shipwreck, journeyings, perils, weariness,
painfulness, hunger, thirst, cold, nakedness, care ". Where was
the comfort that once he knew ? Does not the list make you a
little ashamed, that your Christian adherence causes you so little
distress ? Do you not think that a bit of persecution, in these
days of ease, would perhaps waken us up, tighten us up, smarten
up up into something nearer to the virility of the first believers ?
He had lost great reputation—the Scribes of the day would look
upon this brilliant young man as one of the most promising of
their coming leaders ; he would be held in high esteem by all
who recognised the values belonging to the upright Jewish faith.
Now he is regarded, and treated, as " the off-scouring of the
earth ". Yes, he had lost everything that he had held dear.
How did he view all that sacrifice ? Let Hudson Taylor, founder
of the China Inland Mission, reply, for he experienced something
at least of Paul's troubles. Someone, trying to be encouraging,
said to him, " Mr. Taylor, you must have sacrificed much ".
To which the old missionary veteran replied, " Man, I never
made a sacrifice in my life ". That is just how Paul would have
answered. " Sacrifice ? No, no ; ' for CHRIST ' " (7), on the
other side of the scale, the other side of the account, with all
His treasure, completely outweighed the seeming loss of things.
Florence Nightingale gave it as the secret of her life, " I have
never refused GOD anything "—she gave Him her all. 'Twas no
loss for her, for GOD will be no man's debtor : He countered by
giving His all to her. You see, others than Paul, have had their
strange Profit and Loss Accounts.

" I count all things but loss " (8)—all those things that the
Jewish world estimated so highly. Even the good things, he
rated as of no account seeing that they yielded no interest in the
money-market of the soul, paid no dividends to the " treasury
in heaven ", Matthew vi. 20. Even those things that may
legitimately be reckoned good, the positions and pleasures of

life, the things that " He hath given us richly to enjoy ", this man is gladly willing to forgo, that he throw his whole being into the joyful and fruitful service of his Master. " To what purpose is this waste ", Matthew xxvi. 8, said the disciples, egged on by the money-grubbing Judas, John xii. 6, at the prodigality of a devoted woman's love-gift. They said the same thing when George Pilkington, leading classical scholar of his year at Cambridge, threw up all his fine prospects at home to devote his life to missionary service in Uganda—but what an income accrued from such a loss. They said the same thing when C. T. Studd, Cambridge and England cricketer, gave away his considerable private fortune, and went off to labour in the mission-fields of inland China, and unevangelised Africa—his earthly waste was heavenly winnings. They would have said the same when the attractive little corn of wheat fell into the ground and died ; but " if it die, it bringeth forth much fruit ", John xii. 24. So found Paul—and many more ! Now, therefore, consider—

THE GAINS THAT REVOLUTIONISED THE ACCOUNT

Shall we call the first *a Personal Gain*—" that I may win CHRIST " (8). The word " win " is unfortunate—not by any merits, or deeds, or promises can we win Him : the word should be " gain ", as R.V. All financial gain, all material gain, all physical gain, all intellectual gain, all moral gain, all religious gain—all these are but such little gains compared with the Great Gain. This is a matter of personal choice : we may choose to have Him, or we may refuse to have Him. Back of our choice there is, of course, His sovereign will and grace—" ye have not chosen Me, but I have chosen you. . . ." John xv. 16. They had, indeed, chosen Him ; but, primarily, the choice was His—is always His ; in our case, too. The first entry, because fact, on the credit side of his account is this personal Gain of CHRIST —not any thing, nor any experience, nor any blessing ; it is He alone that can satisfy. And how gloriously He does !

Shall we call the second *a Positional Gain*—that I may " be found in Him " (9). Here we touch on one of Paul's outstanding themes ; over and over again we have the phrase " in CHRIST ", or " in Him ", or " in the Lord ". All that we are, we are because of our position ; all that we have, we have because of our position ; all that we know, we know because of our position ; all that we gain, we gain because of our position. " In Him ", amongst much else, we have a " righteousness ", a right standing before

6

GOD—not derived from any merit of " mine own ", a law-righteousness, arising from scrupulous observance of all its regulations : a pretty hopeless proposition. Ours is, in fact, the spotless righteousness of CHRIST, reckoned to be ours in response to our " faith " in Him ; and followed by a righteous behaviour, that becomes those who enjoy such a position " in Him."

Shall we call the third *a Potential Gain*—big with potentiality, emanating from those two previous gains. (*a*) " *That I may know Him* " (10). Having gained Him, and being found in Him, it is only to be expected that we should have a great desire to come to know Him better and better as the days go by. Knowledge of all kinds, except knowledge of evil, is of great value ; but what knowledge could be compared, either for beauty, for satisfaction, or for power, with this growing intimacy with Him. Abraham was what he was, because he came to be the friend of GOD ; Moses did what he did, because he talked with GOD face to face ; they knew GOD. And, says the old prophet, " The people that do know their GOD shall be strong, and do exploits," Daniel xi. 32. Let us, then, join the apostle in so great a desire ; and let us, by regular communion with Him over the Word, the Footstool, and the Table, and by a daily habit of obedience to His will, seek this wondrous personal knowledge of Himself, which He is so graciously willing to grant to any of His children. (*b*) *And that I may know* " *the power of His resurrection* ". Romans v. 9 says that " *by His blood*, we shall be saved from wrath "—released from all that is meant and involved in sin's guilt, penalty, stain, by His Cross. Romans v. 10 says that " being reconciled, we shall be saved *by His life* "—that is, our ability to conquer sin's daily habit, and our possibility of living in daily holiness, are derived from the power within us of His risen life. " I live, yet not I, but CHRIST liveth in me ", Galatians ii. 20. (*c*) *And that I may know* " *the fellowship of His sufferings* ". CHRIST'S sufferings preceded His resurrection ; Paul's sufferings followed his knowledge of the resurrection. Do you recall Acts ix. 16, after his knowledge of the Risen Lord, " I will show him how many things he must suffer for My Name's sake ". He had essayed to stamp out the Name ; now he must suffer in proclaiming the same. Being ready, if needs be, to suffer for allegiance to Him is a sure test of our love, and a clear mark of our loyalty. And if such experiences are ordained for us, we shall enjoy a very sweet fellowship in them with the Greatest Sufferer of all. (*d*) " *Being made conformable unto His death*." That means, I think, the crucifixion of self, in application of the truth of Galatians ii. 20, Gk., " I have been crucified with

CHRIST ". Yet, the thought of physical death was probably not altogether absent from the apostle's mind for he goes on (e) " *If by any means I might attain unto the resurrection of the dead* " —although even that could refer to the living of the resurrection life here and now, " Nevertheless I live," Galatians ii. 20. " If ye then be risen with CHRIST," Colossians iii. 1. The doctors disagree !

So the apostle escapes his threatened spiritual bankruptcy. Reviewing, with new understanding, his assets and liabilities, his income and expenditure, he closes his Account with a huge Balance on the right side—a Balance at the Bank of Heaven, for sure keeping, Matthew vi. 20 ; and a Balance in Hand to meet daily expenses, or emergencies. When the late Sir Leo Page resigned the honorary secretaryship of a charitable fund connected with the criminal courts in Berkshire, he sent the account books to his successor, accompanied by some lines of verse that he wrote, ending with the thought,

> " When I advance with faltering feet
> To show my final Balance Sheet "

A friend of his, writing in a *Times* obituary, 3 September 1951, says, " His account is in order ". So was Paul's ; and so " in CHRIST " may ours be.

XI

A SPORTING INTERLUDE

PHILIPPIANS iii. 12–16

HERE is this master of illustration at it again, drawing his lessons this time from the Sporting Arena—either, as he is writing from that city, the Roman Stadium ; or, more likely, as the readers would know it better, from the Greek arena of the Isthanian Games. He naturally begins with—

THE START OF THE RACE

" I am apprehended of CHRIST JESUS " (12). How well we know the story of the morning and manner of his arrest on the Damascus road—that was what started him on the Christian race. He was quick off the mark, as all successful athletes must be ; for it says that " *straightway* he preached CHRIST ", Acts ix. 20. It seems a mere cliché to say that we must begin at the beginning ; we cannot barge into the race some laps in front of the starting-point, just wherever we like. Yet, there are folk who do make this mistake. They imagine that to begin the Christian life they must do good things, turn over a new leaf, try their hardest, make solemn promises—all good in their right place, after the race is begun ; but the start is at the point of CHRIST'S grasp of us in grace, and our grasp of Him by faith. Do you remember in John Bunyan's immortal allegory that the Christian way opened at the little Wicket Gate—picture of our Lord JESUS, who said, " I am the door : by Me if any man enter in, he shall be saved ", John x. 9 ; and how that two men, Formalist and Hypocrisy, thinking they knew better, instead of going right round to the starting-gate, climbed over the wall, well ahead of where they should have begun. They were, of course, disqualified.

Have you started yet ? You say, " I go to church "—fine. " I read my Bible "—good. " I say my prayers "—excellent. " I live a decent life "—of course. " I try to help other people " —splendid. I can imagine Nicodemus claiming all this, and more ;

but, as we saw in an earlier study, our Lord told him he had not started yet, John iii. 7. Have you started ? Many of my readers can remember their " Damascus Road "—the place where CHRIST met them, the living JESUS arrested them. Sometimes, that " road " has been a strange place—in my own experience, one was under a street lamp-post ; another was literally on a rubbish-heap ; another was on a seat on Liverpool Street Station, in London. Others, of course, have been in ordinary places : church, chapel, hall, drawing-room, open-air meeting. Where was your starting-place ? How Paul loved to tell of his conversion—dwelling on all the details, amazed at the forgiving love for sinners, " of whom I am chief ", I Timothy i. 15. So he was " apprehended ". It was CHRIST who took the initiative—pricking his conscience, Acts ix. 5, pursuing him along the road, like Francis Thompson's " Hound of Heaven ", persuading him with the urgency of the telegrammatic double-knock, " Saul, Saul " ! No, he could not get over the wonder of it all. When Hebrews xii. 1–2 talks about the Christian Race, it speaks of the Lord JESUS as " the author and finisher of our faith " race. I wonder if we are, on account of the context, justified in interpreting that as " the starter and judge "—fulfilling a double rôle, sending us off from the mark, and welcoming us at the tape. A double rôle would be nothing foreign to Him who is both GOD and man, who is both High Priest and Victim. Anyhow, in fact, even if not in these words, He is both starter at the beginning, and Judge at the finish. So Paul is off !

THE COURSE OF THE RACE

He had not yet finished—" not as though I had already attained " (12). Later on, we find him within sight of the tape, and, in glad anticipation, he says, " I have finished my course ", II Timothy iv. 7 ; but he is not yet there, he has still a long way to go. From the superior manner in which some Christians behave, you might imagine that they had got there—it appears that they have nothing more to experience, nothing more to do, nothing more to learn : they know it all ! They remind me of a boy of fourteen, who, explaining why he had left school, told me, " They can't teach me any more ". Perhaps he spoke more truly than he meant—not that he was so full of knowledge, but that he was so dull that they had given it up. He intended the first : I suspected the latter ! Our apostle had no such delusions—there were gaps yet to be bridged, laps yet to be covered ; there were depths of experience yet to be sounded, heights of attainment yet to be achieved, ere the close of the contest. Meanwhile—

He would not stop still—" I follow after " (12). It is now almost universally questioned if Paul wrote the Epistle to the Hebrews ; but of this there is no question, that he would heartily endorse the sentiment of vi. 1, " let us go on ". He had fully and firmly grasped the fact that conversion was, as we have seen, a starting-place, not a stopping-place. He would have appreciated that, though the seemingly impassable, impossible, Red Sea be in front, the command still holds, " Go forward ", Exodus xiv. 15. There is a place for " Stand still " (verse 13), but no room for standstill—need for quiet, to get new vision, but only for the purpose of preparation for the resumption of the journey. This race is not just a sprint—a quick, brisk burst of energy, and done with. In that case, many more would have succeeded. It is the distance that has beaten ; they could have managed a spurt ; but the keeping on keeping on has proved too much for them. Says Hebrews xii. 1, It is a long-distance race—" let us run with patience ". Says Galatians v. 7, it is an obstacle race —" ye did run well ; who did hinder you ? " Here, in Paul, is an athlete who will not be hindered, not be stopped, but will " go on unto perfection ".

He would put everything into it—" This one thing I do " (13). There is no " I do " in the Greek, so that the broken sentence recaptures the excitement of the apostle in his prison as, in imagination, his heart is pounding at his ribs, as his feet are pounding on the track. He has one over-mastering passion, to the exclusion of all other interests—to get there, and to get there fast. I will not say, to get there first—because I think that this is not a competitive race. Mark his concentration. " Forgetting those things which are behind "—no race could be successful for a contestant who was continually looking back. Old sins—" their sins and their iniquities will I remember no more ", when they are pardoned ; why, then, should we be for ever digging them up, and pining for them ? Former failures—how discouraging they can be ; don't be for ever doing nothing because you were once doing badly. Learn what lessons your failures can teach you, and then forget them. Past experience—some people are perpetually living on the past ; they received a great blessing, perhaps at Keswick, years ago ; let God be thanked for that ; but, alas, these folk never seem to have any fresh, up-to-date blessing to recount. One-time pleasures—that, for whatever reason, they have felt urged to renounce ; but they are, so wistfully, often thinking back to those jolly times of yesteryear.

Like Israel of old—" we remember the fish which we did eat in Egypt freely ; the cucumbers, and the melons, and the leeks, and the onions, and the garlick ; but now . . . there is nothing at all, beside this manna ! ", Numbers xi. 5–6. Some Christians, who once were so happy with " this Manna ", have allowed their appetite for the things of GOD to be spoiled, and now they look back to the old days and pleasures. To all such we would say, " Remember Lot's wife ". Previous successes—these also should be forgotten, for it is ever a temptation to be content with that triumph, to rest on our oars. What a lot of things there are, bad and good, for us to forget ! The Psalmist says, " My times are in Thy hand "—leave your past time there ; and know that " the best is yet to be."

Ponder this, too. " Reaching forth unto those things which are before." Have you ever seen a runner, straining every nerve to maintain, or increase, his speed ? There he is, at full stretch ! That is the picture here. Grasping every opportunity of service, that he may do all he can for GOD, ere the race is done ; seeking to make progress in grace, ever advancing in the things of GOD, that He, our Divine Trainer, may not be disappointed in His protégés ; eagerly anxious to step into all the promises of blessing, longing to apprehend all that GOD purposed in apprehending him (12). Here is a runner in dead earnest ; here is running that makes big demands. The other classic racing passage, Hebrews xii. 1–2, gives sound advice to those who would " run well "—amongst other tips, these. (1) " Let us lay aside every weight "—this last is a medical word, making the phrase to mean, " let us get rid of every ounce of superfluous flesh ", which is just what an athlete does, training down to the last ounce, or, in spiritual parlance, reducing the " I " to the least minimum, as little of self as must be. (2) " Let us lay aside . . . the sin that doth so easily beset us "—that doth so easily wrap us round. The athlete is careful to throw off everything that he decently dare, so that no vestige of unnecessary clothing shall impede him. How often a Christian's progress is slowed down by some besetting (wrapping round) habit of sin. (3) " Looking unto JESUS "—not looking back at the past, as we have seen ; not looking round at others. Like Peter, " What shall this man do ? " and JESUS' reply, " What is that to thee, follow thou Me ", John xxi. 21–2. Our attention wholly given to Him : what is His will in everything ? What will please, and honour Him ? All that need be added is the word Paul sent to the Christian athletes of Corinth, I Corinthians ix. 24, " So run that ye may obtain ", which brings us to—

The End of the Race

" I press toward the mark for the prize of the high calling of
God in Christ Jesus " (Gk.).   The apostle is now looking toward
the finish of the contest, the scene at the tape is, in anticipation,
before his eyes, those last few yards call out all he has in him.
Let us divide up this interesting sentence, and examine it piece
by piece.

" *The mark* "—that is A.V. and R.V. ; but does this translation represent Paul's idea.   On first thoughts it seems easy
to interpret it as referring to the tape at the end of the course,
at whose breaking the prize-winner will be known and acclaimed.
That is the way in which it has been mostly understood.   But
let me put to you a suggestion which has been brought to my
notice by the Rev. A. Cochrane, my old friend and vicar.   In
an old commentary of more than a hundred years ago (1839),
by a Dr. MacKnight, the following suggested rendering is offered,
" I follow in the course *along the mark* ", and, by way of interpretation, it is added, " I run on *the marked-out course* of faith
and holiness ".   Mr. Cochrane proceeds, " So Paul says, in effect,
' I am pressing on towards the Prize to be given when the Race
is finished and won, and I keep to the marked-out Track, as I
must, for the rules must be followed.   If a man strive for
masteries, yet is he not crowned, except he strive lawfully ',
II Timothy ii. 5.   It is the only way, and do you follow my
example, and that of others, who do as I do.   He must keep
pressing on along the marked-out Track."   A most interesting
suggestion.   If you have attended an athletic meeting, you will
have noticed how the track is marked out with lines for the
Hundred Yards, and how each competitor is allotted his lane,
and is bound to keep within those two lines of his track.   That
track is symbolical of the " narrow way ", Matthew vii. 14,
the Way of Faith and Holiness—we cannot go where we like,
we must keep to the appointed track, or we become " a castaway ",
I Corinthians ix. 27 : turned out of the race, not turned out of
the family.

" *The prize* "—it is not competitive, for if I get it, the others
are not deprived of it, as in an ordinary race, wherein " one
receiveth the prize ", I Corinthians ix. 24.   In the Christian
race, all may receive it if they " so run ".   Paul *doesn't despise
the prize*—as some affect to do.   These superiors say that they
do not race, work, serve for reward.   Who does ?   It is " the love
of Christ constraineth us ", II Corinthians v. 14.   But that does
not mean that we will think lightly of it, if we are awarded it,

Our Lord Himself often, shall I say, recommends it, Luke xix. 17 ; Matthew xxv. 21. Who am I to despise it ? The apostle was not ashamed to go all out for it. Paul *doesn't describe the prize*— we know that (*a*) it is not Salvation, being given only to those who have previously got salvation ; (*b*) it is not Heaven, for that is not a prize for our effort, but a gift to our faith. Let us be content to leave it as yet revealed. At least we do know what will be the gracious words that will accompany the presentation— those words, all the more heart-warming as coming from His lips, " Well done ! " It is always an encouragement to get that bit of praise from anyone, but how incomparable the sweetness when coming from Him. That will be worth all the sacrifice, all the striving, all the strenuousness. God help me—help you— so to run as to obtain that distinction, Heaven's medal of the " W.D. " : " Well done ! "

" *The High Calling* "—I have long felt that this should be rendered " the upward calling ", and that it refers to the time of our Lord's return, to call His church up to Himself, as pro- phesied in I Thessalonians iv. 17. It would appear that it is at this dramatic occasion that the judgment seat of CHRIST—the examination of believers' records—is to be set up, in accordance with I Corinthians iii. 12–15, when " reward ", and " loss ", shall be assessed. I have quite recently discovered that my view of this is not new, as I impudently imagined, but that actually it was held by no less a person than Chrysostom, all those centuries ago, who remarked that " athletes are not crowned in the race- course below ; the king calls them up and there crowns them ". At the close of our English football Cup Final, the players of the winning team are called up to receive the Cup, and both teams the medals, from the hands of the Queen, or other High Personage, who has been watching the match from a box above the tiers of seats below. So was it at the Athenian Games, that the Philippians would know so well, that the successful com- petitors were called up to receive their amaranthian crown from their Ruler's hands. So, we believe, will it be at the time when our Lord returns. Those who have gained the prize will have " the upward calling ", to receive from His hands the token of His grace and pleasure, and to hear His wondrous commendation, " Well done "—perhaps, also, the delighted plaudits of the assembled saints. The Parousia will be our prize-giving ! Oh, happy day—if we have " so run ".

" *In Christ Jesus* "—yes, again comes the so-oft repeated emphasis, all is from Him, and in Him. It is His grace that gives us the urge, and the chance, to run, as we " enter " for

the race by the " strait gate " ; it is His grace that gives us
strength to run, and even guidance to run well ; it is His grace
that gives us the prize for good running. He was the " Author "
—the Starter who sent us off ; He is the " Finisher "—the
Judge who holds out to us the incorruptible crown at the end.
Therefore, as the old hymn invites and incites us—

> " Run the straight race, through GOD's good grace,
> Lift up thine eyes, and seek His face.
> Life, with its way, before us lies,
> CHRIST is the Path, and CHRIST the Prize."

Verily, in Him is our protection, our provision, our progression,
and our preoccupation all the way along. Thus, as we saw earlier,
we shall run " looking unto JESUS " for everything needful for
our Christian athleticism—what more inspiring motto could we
have. One further section of the passage now claims our attention. I shall call it—

THE LAGGARDS OF THE RACE

Perhaps we might first consider *the " thus minded " of verse* 15.
Those who share the same mind with Paul on the matters he has
been placing before them. He claims for such that they are
" perfect ". You will notice that he has already used the word
in verse 12—only, in that verse, he is thinking of final perfection,
" not as though I . . . were already perfect ", as though he
were at the perfected end, he would have no patience with the
idea of " sinless perfection " in the present sphere ; while, in
verse 15, he is speaking of the perfection of the intermediate
stage. Of a little baby child you exclaim, " Isn't he perfect ? "
Yes, for his age and stage. You meet a fine, clean, healthy,
upstanding fellow, and you remark to your companion, " Isn't
he a perfect specimen of young manhood ? " Yes, for his age
and stage : but he has a long way to go yet—unless he grows,
he will not be counted perfect of adult middle-age. You come
across an old gentleman, kindly, unselfish, helpful, wise, sunny
—and someone says, " What a perfect old dear ". Yes, for his
age and stage. Down again on the running-track, final perfection
of the sprint is, let us say, one hundred yards in ten seconds.
(As a matter of fact the time has been reduced by a decimal
point or so ; but let us, for the illustration, abide by the ten
seconds.) You stand with stop-watch in hand, and you gauge
him at ten yards in one second—perfect : not final, but stage,
perfection. So he goes on, perfect at each ten yards' stage ;

until, at the end of the hundred yards, he has reached final perfection at ten seconds. So is it with the New Testament, it is relative. When our Lord says, " Be ye therefore perfect, even as your Father which is in heaven is perfect ", Matthew v. 48—He does not mean that we are expected to attain Divine perfection ; but that we are to be perfect in our sphere, and stage, as GOD is in His. If, then, we are to be of such a mind, we shall have to be always at full stretch—no lingering, no loitering, no lagging behind !

Now for *the " otherwise minded " of verse* 15. These are the laggards of the race. They have not the same mind as Paul about it all ; they just don't agree with him. Why all this hurry and energy ? They are in the race—why worry ? They expect to get there in the end. It is all very well to be a Christian ; but why overdo it ? Hold yourself in ; don't make yourself an uncomfortable nuisance to other people—whose unsatisfactory life will be shown up, if you are too religious. Church, yes— but no open-air meetings, no tracts, no prayer-meetings, no personal tackling, no narrow-minded taboos. How shall we deal with such laggards ? The apostle tells them, " GOD shall reveal even this unto you "—that is, will show you how well-worth- while the " all-out " Christian life is, and what a mistake they make who " go slow " ! Rather, let all His athletes not be con- tent with what they have " already attained " (16), but carry on with the same rule, and mind, until the Happy Ending.

XII

HEAVEN BELOW

PHILIPPIANS iii. 17–21

A ONE-TIME famous China medical missionary, Dr. Duncan
Main, was told that the Chinese equivalent of his name was
" Dr. Apricot, of Heaven Below ". That second part is, according
to our passage, applicable to every Christian—he, she, is of
Heaven Below, for " our conversation [our citizenship] is in
heaven " (20). It may be our benediction to have the promise
fulfilled to us, " That your days may be , , , as the days of
heaven upon the earth," Deuteronomy xi. 21. A bit of heaven
here ! Note then, to begin with—

THE CITIZEN LIKENESS

In this happy letter, Paul seems to be anxious to teach the
readers, not only by plain statements of truth, but by illustrations
of the truth, drawn from all quarters of human experience—
for instance, from the banking world, and from the sporting
arena, and now from political life. We recall that Philippi was
a Roman Colony, a bit of Rome away from Rome, its citizens
were citizens of Rome. In those days of Imperial Rome, it was
a thing of enormous pride to be a Roman citizen. After Paul's
Sermon on the Stairs, he escaped scourging by his claim to that
exalted citizen rank, and whereas the chief captain said, " With
a great sum obtained I this freedom," Paul was privileged to be
in a position to say, " But I was free born," Acts xxii. 28. Cities
were sometimes accorded this honour, as well as individuals ;
and for the cause of Philippi's proud position I refer you to my
note under the " Dwelling-Place of the Christians " in the first
Study of this Epistle. How well, then, this city would understand the allusion of this apostle. It is interesting to mark that
it was at Philippi that Paul first used his right of Roman citizenship, Acts xvi. 37.

Here we are, then, in this world, but not of it, John xvii. 16.

We don't belong here ; we are sojourners and pilgrims just journeying through,

> " And nightly pitch my moving tent
> A day's march nearer home.

for, as another hymn says, so accurately picking up the Scripture allusions,

> " I am a stranger here,
> Heaven is my home."

Many a Britisher, settled in Australia, still calls England " home ". Many a citizen of London is serving somewhere abroad, feeling little " at home " there, is often thinking of the affairs and friends from whom, and from which, he is temporarily separated, and looking forward with keen anticipation to the time when he shall get home to the life and loved ones of his real city and country. So it is written, " But now they desire a better country, that is, an heavenly," Hebrews xi. 16, and " he looked for a city which hath foundations [no dream-city, figment of imagination ; but real, and founded upon glorious fact], whose builder and maker is GOD ", Hebrews xi. 10. That city colours all life along the road thitherward. So the Christian is given here the likeness of an absentee citizen. Wherefore consider—

THE CITIZEN LIFE

The apostle has already referred to it when, in i. 27, he said, " Only let your conversation [your citizen behaviour] be as it becometh the gospel of CHRIST ". The citizen of the swell part must not live a slum life. Much of our present passage is given up, negatively or positively, to an examination of what we should live like.

The True Citizens—are in iii. 17. Don't miss the point that they are " Brethren . . . together ". It was a lovely feature of the first generation of Christians that " all that believed were together ", Acts i. 44. There was a grand togetherness—in the faith they held, in the message they proclaimed, in the unity they demonstrated, in the love they practised, in the aim they pursued, in the zeal they showed. Don't we miss that happy sense of togetherness in the church of this generation ? Not looking too far, is this a characteristic of your own particular church—or are there cliques and factions among your members ? Is there an aloofness, a coldness there ? Is there a warm-hearted, family spirit in the congregation ? If not, are you one of the culprits ? Your church will never have the richness of blessing that GOD wants you to enjoy unless, and until, you get "together". We are in the Family together : why, then, should there not be an exhibition of the family spirit in a mutual love and unity together. Do you recall how Psalm cxxxiii. 1 says, "Behold, how good and how pleasant it is for brethren to dwell together in unity!" Notice how the brief Psalm concludes (3), "for there the Lord commanded the blessing". Where there is togetherness, there is blessing. Paul now goes on to tell these Philippian believers that Christian citizens are noteworthy for their capacity for following. Citizens of Scotland in Dunedin, New Zealand, will doubtless follow much of the custom of the Old Country—perhaps they still take salt to their porridge ? Citizens of London, residing for business purposes in Siam, will follow still some of the characteristic colloquialisms and mannerisms of their cockney source. Citizens of Rome would follow the order and habits and outlook of Imperial Headquarters wherever they were situated. You would recognise a Roman centurion anywhere, even when he was in mufti. So it is with the people we are specially considering here : the Citizen of Heaven should follow heavenly ways. Paul bids his Philippians follow (a) "Me" —does that sound egotistic ? I should be surprised if he meant it so. Rather would I think it well to place it alongside of such statements as "Not I, but CHRIST", in Galatians ii. 20 ; and "Not I, but the grace of God", in I Corinthians xv, 10. It is only in that spirit of real humility that this man urges his friends to follow. Moreover, he seems immediately to tone it down by recommending them to take (b) "Us"—for an example. Is this just what we call an editorial plural ? Perhaps ; or, possibly, he is including with himself such people as Timothy, Epaphroditus, and Luke, as fellow-exemplaries. All of these were well known in the Philippian church ; and the apostle may well have pointed to them as good examples of the way that citizens should behave. Take note, he says, of other professing Christians, and see if they come up to the standards that these leading believers set. "Mark them which walk"—that sloucher, and that soldier—and pattern your own carriage accordingly ; for surely it is the vigour and uprightness of the military way that you will desire to emulate, as is becoming to those who bear the proud title of the Citizen of Heaven. One's mind goes back to this same Paul on the shipwreck. A fine upstanding Roman centurion is on board with him, bearing himself with pride, even in the midst of the tempestuous conditions, as the conscious representative of his Emperor. Yet, there is a prouder man there even than Captain Julius, it is Paulos, "little" Paul : listen to him, and catch the tone of pride in

his voice, " GOD, whose I am, and whom I serve," Acts xxvii. 23.
Follow " me ", he now says, follow " us ", who seek to walk as
true and keen representatives of our Heavenly Master. It is
impossible to leave this theme without recalling what he said
of other Christians, that they followed (c) " The Lord "—" ye
became followers of us, and of the Lord ", I Thessalonians i. 6.
So close were these leaders to their Lord that, to follow them was,
almost automatically, to follow Him. How magnificent a claim :
could we possibly make it ? That if they followed us, they would,
ipso facto, be following the Lord ?

The False Citizens—are in iii. 18–19. (*a*) *Their profession*—
was evidently that they were Christians ; but they were not true,
not sincere ; indeed, they were " enemies " in disguise. Open
enemies, scorners, are bad enough ; but I feel sure that they do
less harm to the cause of CHRIST than those who pretend to be
on His side, who for some material, or social, gain masquerade
as believers, while all the while despising the whole business.
" Wolves in sheep's clothing ", our Lord described them. Dogs
and pigs pretending to be sheep ; but, sooner or later, proved by
their backsliding to have been never sheep at all, says II Peter
ii. 22. What damage such people do to the Lord's name and
honour. People of the world take them at their own estimation,
and when their conduct contradicts their profession, when they
are thus " found out ", the worldlings say that all these Christians
are hypocrites and their religion is no earthly use. They fail to
differentiate between the False Citizens and the True Citizens.
(*b*) *Their End*—" is destruction ". Alas, they have turned many
away from the faith because of their behaviour. Many who might
have joined us on the Narrow Way have been discouraged, and
have elected to remain with the majority, Matthew vii. 13, on
their sad way to destruction. Now these false friends themselves
traverse the dark road to their proper end, even as Judas went
" to his own place ", Acts i. 25. What a false citizen that man
was ! (*c*) *Their god*—" is their belly ". While most eat to live,
these live to eat. To satisfy their physical appetite, and, indeed,
their sensual, lustful appetite, is all they care for. After all,
your " god " is the thing, or person, that comes first in your
thoughts, that you most want to please ; and the belted portion
of their anatomy occupies the place of a deity with quite a
number of folk. These here are among these worshippers. F. B.
Meyer told the story of a man of wealth who was taking his
friend round his magnificent mansion, in which a spacious
chamber was dedicated to be a chapel. The visitor, who thought
of little else than good living, on entering the chapel, said, " What

a magnificent kitchen this would make ". Whereupon his host
replied, " You are mistaken, this is not a kitchen ; when I have
made my belly my god, then I will make my chapel my kitchen,
but not before ". Applying the story to " many " whose one
thought is food and drink, Dr. Meyer's comment was, " There is
no chapel in their life, it is all kitchen ". (d) *Their shame*—
" whose glory is in their shame ". That is, they glory in things
of which they ought to be ashamed. As Plummer puts it, " their
boasted liberty was shameful slavery to lust ". There are in
every age, perhaps in every country, those who wickedly make
game of shame. Such people swarmed in parts of Rome, from
which Paul was writing. It is not to be necessarily implied that
persons described in these verses 18–19 were to be found in the
ranks of this Philippian church, though it might be true in Rome,
Romans i. 21–32. The apostle is only concerned to warn his
friends because corruption, like dry rot, has an extraordinary
quality of spreading ; and, as a Latin author put it, " The
corruption of the best is the worst ". Let all Christians beware :
" let him that thinketh he standeth take heed lest he fall ".
(e) *Their mind* " who mind earthly things ". Like John
Bunyan's Man with a Muck-rake—quite unconscious of the
heavenly messenger holding over his head a golden crown,
because his eyes are on the ground, completely occupied with
the menial task of sweeping together the refuse about him.
If those of our verse were truly Citizens of Heaven, their minds
would have been set on heavenly things. " If ye then be risen
with CHRIST, [The ' if ' does not imply any doubt. The Greek
construction would justify the translation ' Since ye then . . .']
seek those things which are above . . . set your affection on
things above, not on things on the earth ", Colossians iii. 1–2.
What a terrible indictment of human beings—indeed, of professing, though not real, Christians. Paul feels that, in the case
of these Philippians, who have only recently come out of impure
heathendom, the danger of infection was very real. So he has
told them about it " often ", and withal " weeping " (18). The
Cross meant so much to Paul ; and it moves him to tears that
those renegades have so far demeaned themselves as to become
" the enemies of the Cross of CHRIST "—not merely of it, but of
Him. Thomas Kelly was moved to write—

> " We sing the praise of Him who died,
>   Of Him who died upon the cross,
>
> .   .   .   .   .
>
> The sinner's refuge here below,
>   The angel's theme in heaven above."

It was more than the deeply emotional apostle could stand to think of people speaking ill of that, and of Him, he held so dear. What does the Cross, the crucified Lord, mean to us ? We speak not just now of its eternal meanings, of its mighty victories—but of the sheer love there displayed for such undeserving sinners. Shall we let that love now lead us on to speak of—

THE CITIZEN'S LORD

As all Roman citizens owed obedience, loyalty, and allegiance to their Emperor, so do the Heavenly citizens owe the same to Heaven's Lord. This JESUS was " born Saviour ", Luke ii. 11 —and we have [have we ?] accepted Him as *our* Saviour. He was also said to have been " born King ", Matthew ii. 2—have we acclaimed Him as *our* King ? Does He actually rule over everything ?

> " If you do not crown Him Lord of all,
> You do not really crown Him Lord at all."

That is true, isn't it ? Think it out. Put it right. Keep it up.

Let us dwell upon the happy thought of our glorified, and glorious, Lord. And first of (a) *His Coming Return*—" from whence also we look for the Saviour, the Lord JESUS CHRIST " (20). Yes, He is not only " a Saviour ", Luke ii. 11 ; but, as here, " the Saviour ", the only one, " there is none other . . . whereby we must be saved ", Acts iv. 12 ; can you go further and say, " My Saviour ", Luke i. 47 ? Again I press the matter upon you, lest, if His return be near, His coming should find you unprepared to meet Him. Do I seem to detect nowadays, in most unexpected quarters, a newly awakened interest, and even belief, in the Second Advent ? Thank GOD if it be so. Certainly that would happily correspond with the striking emphasis on the subject that we find in the Bible—for, with the one exception of the Atonement, there is no other theme that is so often referred to in Scripture. It ill becomes any citizen, therefore, to omit it from his consideration. What a thrill it would be if, for instance, it were announced to these Philippian Roman citizens that the Cæsar was planning to pay them a visit. Imagine how the streets would be cleaned, the houses decorated, the people prepared. That is what, in joyous reality, is going to happen to those who dwell in Heaven Below—our Saviour, King and Lord is actually coming again. Such is " that blessed [happy] hope " of which Paul writes to Titus (ii. 13). It is an interesting grammatical point that, in our twentieth verse, while " heaven " is

7

in the plural, " the heavens ", " whence ", for " which ", is in
the singular—denoting, perhaps, a specific point in the heavens :
might it be the city gate ? Ye earth-wide citizens, keep your
eyes often on that gate, through which He entered in ascension
glory, Hebrews ix. 24, and from which He will one day emerge
in advent glory. Says one commentator, " Oh ! when will those
pearly gates open ! When will that cavalcade issue forth !
When through the dim haze will the Lord come, riding upon His
white horse, and followed by the army of heaven ". What a
hope ; what a day ; what a scene, what a triumph ; what a
joy ! Oh that, being unafraid, and unashamed, we may be
happily ready to join in the welcome to the Returning King.

There is next to be considered (b) *His Transforming Grace*—
" who shall change our vile body, that it may be fashioned like
unto His glorious body " (21). What amazing changes His
advent will bring about. *Changes in world government*—" Behold,
a King [the coming King] shall reign in righteousness ", Isaiah
xxxii. 1 ; *changes in geographical contour*—" His feet shall stand
in that Day [the coming Day] upon the Mount of Olives, and the
Mount shall cleave in the midst . . . and there shall be a very
great valley, and half of the mountain shall remove toward the
north, and half of it toward the south. . . And it shall be in
that day, that living waters shall go out from Jerusalem. . . .
And the Lord shall be King over all the earth," Zechariah xiv.
4, 8–9 ; *changes in animal characteristic*—" the wolf also shall
dwell with the lamb, and the leopard shall lie down with the kid,
and the calf and the young lion and the fatling together . . .
and the cow and the bear shall feed . . . and the lion shall eat
straw like the ox . . . they shall not hurt nor destroy in all My
holy mountain ", Isaiah xi. 6–7, 9 ; *changes in personal character*
—" we shall be like Him, for we shall see Him as He is ", I John
iii. 2, one of the most amazing changes of all ; *changes in human
bodies*—are the particular alterations here under review. " Our
vile body "—the adjective does not really bear the significance
that we attach to it to-day : " the body of our humiliation "
is more the idea—says Lightfoot, " the body which we bear in
our present low estate, which is exposed to all the passions,
sufferings, and indignities of this life ". It was old Archbishop
Whatley who, when on his death-bed, told his chaplain, reading
the passage to him, to alter the A.V. " vile ", to " the body of
our humiliation " ; and it has been acceptable to the scholars
ever since. This body of ours, then, beset with limitations,
nerves, injuries, is, at His Coming to be completely transformed
to be like " the body of His glory ". Remember the body of

His Transfiguration splendour, the body of His Resurrection wonder, the body of His Ascension beauty—what glory! And my body is to be something, somehow, like that. Amazing! A more detailed examination of the marvel is given in I Corinthians xv.

So we come to (c) *His Almighty Power*—" according to the working whereby He is able even to subdue all things unto Himself " (21). " Able to save ", says Hebrews vii. 25. " Able to succour ", says Hebrews ii. 18. " Able to subdue ", says the verse here. Indeed, there is no limit to what He is able to do for us. Things that can't be can be, if He is there. Look at the Bible Home of Incurables, Mark v. The men's ward contains that poor hopeless, helpless man, Legion—" no man could bind him . . . neither could any man tame him ". Until the Good Physician enters the ward : then the impossible cure is wrought ! The women's ward has a poor, distressed soul—" suffered many things of many physicians, and had spent all that she had, and was nothing bettered, but rather grew worse ". Twelve years already she had suffered. Must she go on like that : can nothing be done for her ? Nothing ! Until He enters, to work the miracle. The children's ward shows us a pathetic case : the little person might have been healed but for the delay in the women's ward. Alas, now she's gone, " thy daughter is dead "—beyond all aid. All aid ? No, not His—for when He enters the mighty deed is done. Tell me, has sin got such a hold of you that yours is a hopeless case ? The devil is strong, but JESUS is stronger— " Satan to JESUS must bow ". Tell me, are you finding life intolerable—so full of difficulty, distress, disappointment ? He is able to subdue that life of yours, so that though you feel like old Jacob, " all these things are against me," Genesis xlii. 36, you yet shall see that " all things work together for good to them that love GOD ", Romans viii. 28.

The citizen's Lord is an almighty Lord, able to subdue their lives, their wills, their circumstances, their bodies, their all— until the blessed day when all the joy of their citizenship shall be finally released, and fully released, in their Homecoming.

XIII

A FLY IN THE OINTMENT

PHILIPPIANS iv. 1–3

THIS passage for our present Study is a very short one, but it is none the less important on that account. So often the little things of Scripture turn out to be big in value. That little word " so " for instance—one of the unfathomed words in the Bible ; " GOD *so* loved . . . ", John iii. 16 : how deep, how high, how wide, how long is that " so " ? That little verse, John xi. 35, " JESUS wept " ; how expressive of His tender compassion concerning the affairs of His friend. That little book Haggai, with its needful message on Work ; or Philemon, with its word to Management and Labour ; or III John, and its dissertation on " How do you do ? ". That little man, Zacchæus, so wondrously converted. Yes, the Bible's little things have a strange way of suggesting the arresting quality of bigness. So we turn to our brief portion, feeling sure that blessedness will be found there. Let us confine our first attention to the first verse ; and for all its sweetness, let us give to it the title of—

THE ODOUR OF THE OINTMENT

We recall at once the lovely incident in the Gospels, one of whose beautiful influences was that " the house was filled with the odour of the ointment ", John xii. 3. There is a like refreshing fragrance in our first verse. This precious nard is compounded of a number of sweet-smelling ingredients—some of which have already claimed our attention.

" *Therefore* "—sending us back to the conclusion of the previous chapter, with its reminder of the all-sufficiency of the power of GOD. How reassuring it is to know that, as the base and basis of this mixture of mercy, we have this strong and all-permeating essence of His might. The scent of it, even by itself, has revived the spirits of many a fast-fainting soul, that from the depths of despondency has been brought back to take on, as it were, a new lease of life. Its detected presence has spurred on many a CHRIST's warrior with a spirit of battle and an assurance of victory.

Power : that is what every earnest Christian is seeking for. His Power : that is what will prove adequate to the answering of every call made upon us. In this Philippian church, a situation has arisen which has so far baffled all attempts to settle it. In all Christian ages, and circles, we find the same problem, equally obstinate of solution ; but let us all be quite certain that, as we saw last Study, nothing is beyond the power of GOD. And to the expectant, obedient, soul there comes again and again the old promise, " Ye shall receive power after that the HOLY GHOST is come upon you ", Acts i. 8—power for witness, power for consistency, power for understanding, power for ministry, power for enthusiasm, power for holiness. I thank GOD that this " Therefore " is present as the very foundation of this unguent.

" *My brethren* "—Paul meant what he said. It is so easy to use the term formally, for a man to call another Christian " brother ", for a minister to address his congregation as " Dearly beloved brethren "—it may be the expression of his real feeling, but it may be sheer, cold, meaningless phraseology. On Paul's lips, as he dictated it to his stenographer, it was real. His chained companion of a Roman soldier would, of course, overhear, and perhaps would wonder at the evident feeling that his prisoner put into his use of the common word. You would imagine that they really were his brothers—as they really were ! For writer and readers were members of a family ; they rejoiced in one Father, and were, therefore, each, brother or sister. It is good to recognise in the make-up of the ointment this delightful component of the Family spirit. Yet, I fancy that this word " brethren " carried for Paul a scent of memory, whose fragrance would never die. Years before he had been a cruel and fanatical persecutor of the Christian faith, till he was " apprehended of CHRIST JESUS " (iii. 12). Blind, alone, dejected, in his Damascus lodging, he was granted a vision of a man coming in to minister to his utter need. What manner of attitude would this Ananias adopt ? Only one was possible in the estimation of this now stricken man—cold, stiff, aloof, revengeful. Saul of Tarsus would know that he deserved it all. And now, at the knock admitting the visitor, the erstwhile persecutor expects the worst ; but Ananias, crossing the room to where the blind man sat, put his hand on him, Acts ix. 17, and said, " Brother Saul. . . ." Brother ? It would almost break the heart of this deeply emotional man. Brother, Brother—he called me Brother ! I suspect that, from that moment it became for him a sacred word ; and when he called others brothers, this was, at least, part of the reason why his use of the name was invested with such sincere meaning.

Do we, I wonder, think of, and treat, our fellow-Christians as real brothers and sisters in CHRIST ? The unbrotherly behaviour of some of us is a scandal to faith, and a denial of citizenship—such is not known in Heaven Above, why, then, in Heaven Below ?

" *Dearly beloved* "—two doses of it, you observe, in this odoriferous ointment of a verse ; and strong doses at that. Not merely love, but dear love ! This is something deeper than brotherliness. Do you recall Peter's Ladder of Christian Character, in II Peter i. 5–7, how we are bidden to ascend rung by rung, thus to " add to " one quality the attainment of the next, beginning, of course, with the step of " faith " ? When we are almost at the top he says, " And to godliness, brotherly kindness ". But we are, even yet, not at the end of the climb ; here it is, " And to brotherly kindness, love ". Yes, I said that love was something deeper than brotherliness—I must add, something higher ! There may be faults and foibles in our brother (as there are in us !), but love can understand, and overlook " love thinketh no evil " of his brother, 1 Corinthians xiii. 5. I love Moffatt's translation of that " doth not behave itself unseemly " in the beginning of that verse 5—he renders it, love " is never rude " ! No ointment of behaviour is " up to proof " unless it have in it a goodly infusion of up-to-standard love. As we said in an earlier Study, Oh, for a baptism of first-century love upon the twentieth-century church. Paul had it, as we see, in full measure.

" *My joy and crown* "—the first, for the present ; the second, for the future. What a delightful perfume of personal appreciation is here added to the compound. Paul was always ready, even quick, to recognise and acknowledge the good in those to whom he wrote, even if there was much in them to reprove ; but to none did he pay such glowing tribute as to these at Philippi, in whom, indeed, he found so little cause for dissatisfaction, or reprimand. They were, almost without exception, such a " joy " to him, as he thought of them, prayed for them, wrote to them. And one day they, with others, would prove a " crown " to all his endeavour—not the " diadema " crown of royalty, but the " stephanos " crown of victory. Have you got a crown coming to you : some whom you have won to CHRIST ? What a joy here ; what a glory hereafter.

" *Stand fast* "—the temptation is to give way. The pressure of a heathen city is very strongly, and very seductively, anti-Christian ; the threat of fierce persecution is even, in those days, to be expected ; the not unnatural tendency to a drop in the temperature of their zeal, owing to the absence of their leader, who meant so much to them, ii. 12. These, and other things, might so easily, if they are off their guard, lure them to backsliding. There is no sign of it, so far, in that happy-spirited assembly of GOD's people ; but it is always salutary to have warning. " I will thank the Lord for giving me warning", says the Psalmist. So this astringent ingredient is included in this prescription. The man of mercury, for ever up and down, in and out, will not be a happy Christian, neither will he be a dependable person in the cause of GOD. As we saw earlier, the Christian race calls for stickers, not sprinters. The satisfactory spiritual life is not governed by the prevailing fashion—he is no chameleon —nor by fears, nor by feelings, but by faith—a whole-hearted trust and reliance, as becomes citizens of a heavenly kingdom. That kingdom will be poorly served by those who, in Meyer's phrases, are " now like a seraph flashing with zeal, now like a snail crawling in lethargy ". So stand fast. Remember the word that CHRIST spoke to one of the earliest of His disciples—" Thou art Simon . . . thou shalt be called Cephas . . . a stone ", John i. 42. May we, too, be transformed (if need be) from the Simon of shifting sand into the Peter of resisting rock.

" *In the Lord* "—ah, there is the secret of steadfastness : " rooted . . . in Him ", as Colossians ii. 7 says. See that great, towering oak. It began its life as a little acorn, shooting down its little rootlet, sending up its tiny spikelet, and gradually, as it grew, taking firmer hold of mother earth, daily giving evidence of its increasing strength, till it becomes the mighty tree before your eyes. How can it so splendidly stand fast ? It is all in the hold. Not just in the tree's hold of the earth, but principally, primarily, in the earth's hold of the tree. In other words, it is not We, but He ! So, to complete the ointment, goes in this oil of dependence on the Lord, binding together all the qualities that constitute its make-up—the brotherliness, the love, the joy, the steadfastness : all are ours, as we are in Him. " Abide in Me, and I in you," John xv. 4. But now, alas—

THE OFFENCE OF THE FLY

This second verse of our passage is such a sad, and bad, contrast to what we have been considering thus far. Two women ! Ah, but they were not the only women in the Philippian church —there was Lydia, Acts xvi. 14, 40, with her quiet acceptance of the Lord JESUS, and her consistent Christian kindliness, sympathy, and hospitality. I wonder how the Church would

have got on without its godly women—the sons they have
trained for her, the services they have rendered for her, the songs
they have written for her, the supplications they have offered
for her—from Eunice's training of Timothy, II Timothy i. 5 ;
iii. 15 ; from Tabitha's originating of the Dorcas meeting, Acts
ix. 36 ; from Mary's song of Magnificat, Luke i. 46 ; from the
women's joining in the Upper Room prayer-meeting, Acts i. 14 ;
from these onward, the Church has owed a debt she can never
adequately repay for all her women's sacrifices, service, and
sympathy.

Here, alas, are two ladies that have fallen out. The pity is
that they are evidently women of standing and influence ; and
certainly they have both been very earnest and energetic in the
work, " women which laboured with me in the gospel " (3), as
Paul testified. And now, comic in Satan's eyes, tragic in ours,
they are quarrelling. As likely as not it will be over some trifling
thing one being preferred rather than the other ; one assuming
a position supposed to belong to the other ; and so, the one
thinking hardly of the other, and the other speaking harshly to
the one. Each imagines the other to be in the wrong—of course,
they both are. They are Christians, if you please, prominent
Christians ; a sad pair, this Euodia and Syntyche. They are
ruining their own happiness, spoiling the Church's gladness,
adding to the devil's joy. And they won't make it up ! They
won't kiss and be friends, as Christian ladies should. Mind you,
it is not always the women that are thus doing such damage to
the Church's blessing and witness. Just as often the culprits are
to be found among the men of the congregation, the Mr. Euodias
and Mr. Syntyches of the company. Two office-bearers who
won't speak to each other—sidesmen who can't stand one
another—deacons who bear each other a grudge. Perhaps they
don't realise that the quarrel is not just between each other, but
is a controversy of each together with GOD—and His blessing
is being held up accordingly : not they only suffer, but the whole
congregation and Church likewise. And they won't make it up !
They won't shake hands and be friends, as Christian gentlemen
should.

Now Paul makes a strong appeal to them, " *I beseech* " ; for
he knows what harm they are doing by their unseemly wrangle.
We don't know what success he had ; we can only hope that he
was able to bring them to " *the same mind* ", that whether it
were some general disagreement, or some personal grievance,
they came to think alike. Of course, that could only come to
pass if one all-embracing secret be embraced, if they settle the

thing "*in the Lord*"—there it is again! They would be likely to arrive at a common understanding, the same mind, if only they would view the matter as in His eyes. Writing to another company of believers, the apostle says, "We have the mind of CHRIST", I Corinthians ii. 16. Ah yes, if each of these two ladies had the mind of CHRIST, they would have the same mind. Simple, isn't it? Most of our personal problems are easily solved "in the Lord". The company of the Church is like to a wheel, whose rim is the circumference of the faith in which all the members are embraced. Those members are the spokes; and if any of them be broken, or get out of place, the strength of the wheel is affected. If, however, all is well, it is found that the nearer they get to the axle, the nearer they get to one another. That axle is CHRIST, and "in Him" the members discover their unity, and the welfare of the whole community. Take heed, ye estranged ladies, or gentlemen; and take heart, ye troubled Church. For you have your part to play in bringing about this happy solution.

THE OBLIGATION OF THE OTHERS

There is an interesting change of word used here, in our third verse. To the ladies, Paul used a word for "beseech" which almost amounted to a command; to these others, the word translated "entreat" asks, as of a friend, a favour. Will these who are now addressed take up this problem as a matter of personal obligation? The quarrel of any two members of a church really should be a concern to the others—we are to try to "help those" who are estranged to come to that "same mind" we spoke of. It will need courage, often; it will call for infinite tact; it will most certainly require prayer, much prayer; and, make careful note of this, it must be attempted in no spirit of superiority, or condemnation, but in a real spirit of love. With these, perchance, the reconciliation may be brought about. But we ourselves must be "in the Lord", in harmony with His mind.

Who are these people here addressed? "*True yokefellow*"—who is he? We do not know; but all kinds of suggestion have been made. The great New Testament scholar, Professor Ramsay thinks it may have been Luke. Others have ventured the opinion that it was Barnabas, Timothy, Silas. There was an early belief that it was the apostle's wife; but surely I Corinthians vii. 8 means that he was either a bachelor, or a widower; and, in any case, surely if he were referring to a wife, he would at least be careful to make the " yoke-fellow " a feminine word, not masculine, as we have it. The same objection applies to Renau's suggestion that it was Lydia. No—if we have got to cast a vote we shall follow Lightfoot, and name Epaphroditus as the person, who is to carry the letter, and is here urged to use whatever influence he may be able to exert to get the parties to agree. But nothing is anything more than mere conjecture. The bishop's chief reason for choosing Paul's postman is that " in his case alone there would be no risk of making the reference unintelligible by the suppression of the name ". And then, " *with Clement also* ", apparently a Christian gentleman, residing at Philippi, who might be supposed to carry some weight when tackling these difficult ladies. There seems little to connect him with the famous early bishop of that name—the only point is that his Letter to the Corinthians was written to heal a feud in a distant but friendly church. We are indebted here again to Bishop Lightfoot. No, he was " Clement of Rome " ; this was " Clement " of Philippi. " *With my other fellow labourers* ", Paul was anxious to enlist the aid of all that he could lay hands on to try to heal the breach—anyone, anything, so long as the scandal is silenced. Such importance does he attach, and that we should attach, to the squalls and squabbles of church members.

And, as Paul closes the paragraph, he gathers all these Christian believers, yes, including Euodia and Syntyche, within the embrace of a truly wonderful and beautiful phrase and fact—" *whose names are in the book of life* ". The old Testament references to such a book are very striking—for instance, Exodus xxxii. 32 ; Psalm lxix. 28 ; cxxxix. 16 ; Daniel xii. 1 ; and when we come over into the New Testament, we find, in the Apocalypse, frequent mention of it—iii. 5 ; xiii. 8 ; xxi. 27 ; xxii. 19. Such continuous allusion would suggest that there is something more than mere metaphor here, that there is some substantial fact indicated, some record of names and personalities, inclusion in whose list is eternal joy, and omission eternal woe. Would you like to have a peep at its pages ; or would you be too apprehensive, lest your name were not there ? Some of you will recollect your Final Examination at college, and how the list of passes was posted on the board. You can recapture even now the feeling of dread which prevented you looking, lest your name did not appear. You besought someone else to tell you.

Listen ! If you are a real believer you need have no such qualms and fears concerning this record of heaven's graduates. Revelation xxi. 27 says it is " the Lamb's book of life ". Its lists are composed of the names of those who, by faith, have savingly beheld " the Lamb of GOD, which taketh away the sin of the world ", John i. 29. Inclusion in that Book depends on worth—not our worth, but His. In the old days of France they used to have a record book, something like our own Domesday Book. In it was recorded a note of the taxes due from each city, town, and village—a page for a place. At the page assigned to the little village of Domrémy, there was the list to be paid by it to the government. But across the page, written in red ink, and of course, in French, were the words, " Taxes remitted for the Maid's sake ". Joan of Arc, the maid of Orleans, was born there, and one of the marks of a, then, grateful government, for her military triumph against the invading English, was to honour her native village with this remission in perpetuity. I see a vision of other " books ", Revelation xx. 12. If you could open the volume devoted to the record of my unworthy life, you would find across its pages, written in red, as if with the Blood of JESUS Himself, the words, " Sins forgiven for His Name's sake ", I John ii. 12. Continuing in the metaphor of that Revelation verse, I note that, at that Great White Throne, " the books were opened . . . the dead were judged out of those things which were written in the books, according to their works ". Not my book ; nor yours, if you are a true believer. For when those Red Words cancelled out our " debts ", Matthew vi. 12, that book was closed for ever, and our names were transferred and inscribed in " another book [which] was opened, which is the book of life ". We are not there come up for judgment ! What joy is ours, and what glad thanksgiving.

XIV

ONE HUNDRED PER CENT.

PHILIPPIANS iv. 4–9

SOME of us Christians are only half-and-half ; others are out-and-out. Some are "A.1." ; others are "C.3". Travellers on the Gospel Train can choose which Class they go to Heaven by—Third Class, which means, CHRIST present ; Second Class, which means CHRIST prominent ; or First Class, which means CHRIST pre eminent, Collossians i. 18. Paul is out for the best ; he is all in favour of the first class ; he wants his Philippian converts to be 100 per cent. Christians. So he sets before them, and us, a fourfold ideal of spiritual life. Can it be achieved ? Or, is it too much to expect ? Well, let us study it carefully, and see.

UNFAILING JOY

"*Rejoice in the Lord always : and again I say, Rejoice*" (1) Joy, more Joy, much Joy—yes ; but unfailing joy ? Let us remind ourselves that this is outstandingly the Epistle of Joy—the word "Rejoice" comes no less than eleven times in these four chapters ; and, in addition, the word "Joy" occurs five times. To have such repetition within so small a compass surely gives the tone and tendency of the whole. The writer is not just quoting from a book, nor repeating what someone else has said he has himself this joy in his own heart, and that, be it remembered, in spite of (*a*) his fetters—chained by the wrist all the time to the Roman soldier, who would be amazed at his prisoner's exuberance of spirit, and that he seemed to expect that everybody holding his religious beliefs should be uniformly happy, judging from the things he was dictating in his letter to Philippian Christians. Moreover, his joy was there in spite of (*b*) his future —he was awaiting trial, and knew not how things would go, (ii. 23) ; but whether this, or that, he would "count it all joy", James i. 2. It had been the same when he was actually with them in Philippi. Observe him, with Silas, his back torn and bleeding, his limbs chained to the dank wall of the filthy inner prison.

Now we shall see ! He said " alway "—was he talking rhetoric, or reality ? Listen, " at midnight Paul and Silas prayed, and sang praises unto GOD ", Acts xvi. 25. Ah yes, for him " alway " may stand. We would not allow any man to say " Rejoice alway " to us, who had himself known nothing but sunshine ; but we'll take it from this man Paul. Do you remember, also, how our Lord, in the Upper Room, facing the awful realities of the cup of Gethsemane, the chastisement of Gabbatha, and the cross of Golgotha, yet speaks of " My joy ", John xv. 11. It seems that with the song of joy in our hearts we may move happily along the road of life.

> " There are in this loud, stunning tide
>   Of human care and crime,
> With whom the melodies abide
>   Of the everlasting chime ;
> Who carry music in their heart,
> Through dusty lane and wrangling mart,
> Plying their daily task with busier feet
> Because their secret souls some holy strain repeat."

So wrote John Keble for " St. Matthew's Day ", and how happily appropriate for every day. How great an evangelistic force is this quality of joy—to let the world see and know that there is a fount of joy persisting through the strains and sorrows of life. Gloom is the word that too often we allow the unbeliever to associate with our religion : may we help them to find gladness there instead. We are not to confuse this quality with mere boisterous hilarity. As Paul's friend Seneca once said, " True joy is a serene and sober motion, and they are miserably out that take laughing for rejoicing ". Rejoice in our gifts, our friends, our interests : yes, but even if we lose them all, we may Rejoice " in the Lord "—He is Himself the source of gladness, as of all blessing, as this Epistle is constantly reminding us.

UNENDING SELFLESSNESS

" *Let your moderation be known unto all men* " (5). This " moderation " is given in the Revised Version as " forbearance " ; perhaps an even truer rendering would be " yieldingness ". The Christian art of giving way. Not on principles—one recalls this very apostle writing about the troublesome Judaisers, " to whom we gave place . . . no, not for an hour ", Galatians ii. 5 ; there are some in the Church who are prepared to give everything away for the sake of peace ; by all means, so far as we can, but we must not sacrifice principles. But let us be ready to give up our rights—if, as Christians, we have any ; our pleasures—if they should be a cause of harm to others ; our preferences—if we can thus be a help to someone else. What a difference it would have made if Euodia and Syntyche had displayed this spirit of yieldingness. " Unto all men "—some to whom we are attracted, it would be easy to yield to them, but " all " ? Though Christians, we are yet human ! Ah but, " the Lord is at hand " (5)—therein lies the possibility of the hundred per cent. The phrase does not, I think, here refer to our Lord's Second Coming and its near approach. The apostle is an ardent exponent of that theme elsewhere, but not in this verse. Paul means that his Lord is near by him, with all that His close presence brings. In that prison room where four—Epaphroditus, to whom he was dictating the letter : it was a comfort to have him near ; the soldier, so near that the apostle was chained to him by the wrist with a chain of steel, embarrassingly near ; but Another was nearer still, bound to him with a chain of love—the Lord was at hand, at that same hand as the Roman was. So would Paul find a secret of yieldingness, even to the whims of his irksome companion ; and so would he impress upon us all the duty, and the possibility, of this truly Christian characteristic. We call to mind his saying in verse 5 of his exquisitely beautiful I Corinthians xiii, that " love seeketh not her own ".

UNRUFFLED PEACE

" *The peace of God, which passeth all understanding* " (7). There is a peace which is quite understandable—when the sun is shining, with friends, and comforts, and health, and wealth. This is something so different from that. It is variously described (*a*) As a legacy—" peace I leave with you, My peace I give unto you ", John xiv. 27. Such is a clause in the Master's Last Will and Testament, given on the night before He died. (*b*) As a fruit—" the fruit of the SPIRIT is . . . peace," Galatians v. 22. One of the nine trees is His lovely orchard, whose gates are freely open to His people. (*c*) As a garrison—" shall keep your hearts and minds through CHRIST JESUS ". Shall " garrison ", is the word : a heavenly sentinel challenging the approach of anything that would worry your mind, or disturb your heart. How attractive is this quality of peace in this troubled world, and how effective in the experience of those who know where to find it. As with " My joy ", so now with " My peace ", we marvel that our Lord was able to speak thus in the face of all that immediately confronted Him. The secret lies not with ourselves, but with Him. " Thou wilt keep him in perfect peace [one hundred per cent.] whose mind is stayed on Thee, because he trusteth in Thee ", Isaiah xxvi. 3. I said it is not with ourselves to manufacture this infinitely desirable boon ; yet there are preliminary steps towards it that we alone can take. *Careful for nothing*—" be careful for nothing " (6). Not wrongfully, distrustfully anxious about things. You are His ? Then all your concerns are His care, I Peter v. 7. There is a very illuminating " therefore " in Matthew vi. 25. Our Lord has, in the previous verse, been talking about slavery—to " serve " means to " be a slave "—and He goes on to stress that because we are His slaves, " therefore " all our needs are His responsibility, and we need not be anxious. We enlarged upon the theme in our opening chapter, and need not particularise now—but the fact bears repetition ! *Prayerful for everything*—" in everything by prayer and supplication . . . let your requests be made known unto GOD " (6). " What a privilege to carry everything to GOD in prayer ", as the old hymn says. When difficulties and distresses surround us, how it ministers towards peace to bring it all before Him in prayer. Three different words are used in the Greek of this verse for prayer. The word translated " prayer " is what we may call, Prayer in General. A talking with GOD, quite naturally, about everything—smiling to Him in joy ; confiding in Him in sorrow ; looking to Him for direction ; talking over with Him the details of daily life. May we all learn thus to live in the spirit of prayer. The word for " supplication " may be held to represent, Prayer in Particular. The taking to Him of some specific matter, subject, event, person— whether we intercede alone, or whether " two of you shall agree ", or whether " prayer [is] made of the Church ", as a whole, Acts xii. 5. There is a third word here, rendered " requests ", which we may be allowed to think of as indicating Prayer in Detail. GOD is, so to say, interested in the Telescopic view, things afar, things at large. He is also interested in the Microscopic view, things near by, things minute—the details. Shall we put it, by way of illustration : the Concert as a whole ; the Programme in particular ; the Items in detail. Or, the Men's Meeting in general ; the one Man in particular ; the Many needs he has in detail. We think of George Müller's life of Prayer in general, the Orphanage in particular, the Children's welfare in detail. Thus are we for ever encouraged to bring to GOD the big things, and the little things of life. How powerfully it all contributes to peace and poise. *Thankful for anything*—" with thanksgiving " (6). It is remarkable how remiss we Christian often are about this. It is surely bad manners, to say the least, that we receive so much at GOD's hands without so much as a " Thank You ". We teach our children better than that ; and yet we children of GOD so sadly forget ourselves. A famous hymn tells us to " Count your blessings, name them one by one " —but how long a time it would take us to tot the tally of them. Our positive blessings, so numerous ; our negative blessings, no less—for remember that every misery we haven't got is a mercy we have got. Well, I cannot help feeling that a thankful spirit is a practical contributor to peace. In fact, all these three things are preparatory to this composed state of mind which the hundred per cent. Christian covets earnestly. Having recited them *seriatum*, the apostle proceeds, " and the peace of God . . . shall . . ."

You may say, " You don't know what you are talking about " —perhaps not ; but Paul did. Besides, this is the HOLY SPIRIT inspiring, speaking through him ; and He doesn't mock people. He promises this untroubled calm, because it is a possible experience. In the face of all the anxieties and perplexities of the hour, in spite of all the sorrow, and sickness, and even suffering that may visit your own home—peace ? You can't understand it ? No, neither did Paul, for it is a " peace that passeth all under-standing ". Here it is, then, for our trustful acceptance, whatever the conditions and circumstances—" perfect peace, and at such a time ", Ezra vii. 12.

UNBLEMISHED LIFE

To " think " right (8), *and to " do " right* (9). These comprise the whole of life, and to have these twin-springs pure and sweet is to have the character unsullied, or as James i. 27 would say, " to keep himself unspotted from the world ". We will here begin with *the Thought life*—a strategic point in all being. The apostle does not stay to deal with evil thoughts. Some of our present-day psychologists are, in this particular, almost akin to Keswick teaching and New Testament doctrine ; for these are now saying that if we wish to subdue and conquer evil thoughts, we must, on no account, try to fight them, and thus devote our attention to them. That, these say (and, please, I am speaking only of some), is asking for trouble, and will only aggravate their lure. Paul, then, by the HOLY SPIRIT made wise before his time, urges his readers to take the positive line, and to cultivate the good thoughts. He mentions eight things on which the mind may well concentrate. " *True* "—probably not in the sense of truth, as of " reality ". Paul uses the same Greek word, in the Christian's armour, of being " girt about with truth ", Ephesians vi. 14, where, I think, the same idea is in mind. The first thing a Roman soldier does when buckling on his armour is to girdle up his ordinary garment and thus prepare for the fixing of his arbitraments. He cannot wear them without that. Neither can the Christian soldier wear his unless, and until he is a Christian in reality—only then is he properly caparisoned with the whole panoply of GOD. " Honest "—a difficult word is used, and many renderings have been suggested. I surmise that " honourable " is the likeliest meaning here. " Just " —not merely just in the ordinary, human sense, but " righteous " as in the eyes of GOD. " Pure "—Lightfoot suggests " stainless ". Some thoughts leave a stain, which is difficult enough to erase. " Lovely "—wholly " admirable ", having an innate beauty, all their own. " Of good report "—the idea of this word seems to be " winsome ", having a quality well-reputed, so that such things win not only the approbation but the application of others. " Virtue "—the word so translated is used in II Peter i. 5, " add to your faith virtue . . .", where I would venture the suggestion that, if not the meaning at least the significance, of the word is " consistency " ; and, greatly presuming, I would offer the same rendering here. " Praise "—we may put it as " praise-worthy ", primarily here, in the estimation of men, but we can go beyond that to the reckoning of GOD.

Well, there they are—how purifying, how stimulating, will the dwelling upon such things be. But there is an old saying that " you can't prevent a bird flying over your head, but you can prevent it making a nest in your hair ". So it is with evil thoughts. To take the positive line that Paul here wages will certainly reduce the coming of these unworthy things ; but, when all is said and done, you will find such an enemy aeroplane slipping through occasionally. It is not wrong if they come ; it is only wrong if you harbour them. What shall be done with those stray thoughts of evil, or these wandering thoughts that invade and invalidate even your prayer-time ? The answer is, act the policeman ; which I will explain by referring you to II Corinthians x. 5, " bringing into captivity every thought to the obedience of CHRIST ". If a policeman saw a man unlaw-fully trying to enter a house, he would promptly arrest him in the name of the Queen. That's it ! When that unlawful thought seeks to enter, act instantly, arrest it in the Name of the King— " captivity . . . to be obedience of CHRIST ".

We must turn now, in our consideration of the hundred-per-

8

cent. Christian experience to say something about *the Active life*—this " do " of verse 9. Two avenues for the guidance of their behaviour are suggested. (*a*) Careful instruction—" those things which ye have both learned and received " (9). Paul knew the value of a gospel ministry addressing itself to the heart and will of the hearer, seeking to get a verdict for the Master. But he was careful about the educational, as well as the emotional. When he had got his converts, he was keen about their spiritual advancement, and with them his work became a teaching ministry. Isn't it a fact that there is a woeful lack of teaching in our churches to-day ? Read again the epistles of Paul and see how full they are of massive doctrine—no wonder that there was so little back-sliding among his converts. They not only " learned " it, as a matter of information ; but they " received " it as a matter of personal experience. (*b*) Concrete example— was the second source of their instruction ; " those things which ye have . . . heard and seen in me ". " Heard " about my manner of life when I was absent, " seen " in me when I was present. This presenting of himself as an example of Christian living, to which he refers in several places in the Epistle, must not be misunderstood. It is not to be put down to an exalted opinion of his own goodness. The trouble lay in this, that the New Testament had not yet been written, and though a good deal of oral ministry concerning the life of Christ was extant, anything in the way of a complete picture was not yet available. He left us " an example, that ye should follow His steps ", I Peter ii. 21 —but it was not always easy to see His steps. So, says Paul, follow me, and you will be in the way of following Him. Thus he applies it (*c*) in practical fashion—" those things . . . do " (9). It is not enough to know, we must be sure to do what we know —" if ye know these things, happy are ye if ye do them ", John xiii. 17. I am so often impressed with that " do " in I John i. 6 —" *do* not the truth ". You see, the Truth is not simply something to be discovered, to be understood, to be admired, to be preached—it is something to be done !

The delightful result of all this hundred-per-cent. life is that " the GOD of peace shall be with you " (9). Before, he had said, " the peace of GOD " (7), now, better still, it is " the GOD of peace ". These all-out Christians shall have a new sense of the presence, and power, and purpose of their GOD. Happy people !

XV

ENOUGH AND TO SPARE

PHILIPPIANS iv. 10–20

SUCH was part of the description of the prodigal of his father's home, when he had come to see what a fool he had been, and was reduced to such a state as to " perish with hunger ". Even the slaves back home were in better case than he. They had " bread enough and to spare ", Luke xv. 17. It is a like impression that we get from our passage concerning our Heavenly Father's resources ; and after all that we have learned as to what He expects of His children, it is good to have the assurance that sufficient supplies are available for our strengthening, that we may be, and say, and do all that is required of us. Come, then, to these verses, and see the message they have for us. Consider, first—

THE VARIETY OF NEED

" All your need ", says verse 19—" every kind of need, material and spiritual ", is Plummer's comment. A good deal is said about *the Material needs*. Since the time when he became a Christian, Paul had often been in want, but he didn't talk about it—" not that I speak in respect of want " (11). He had learned a great lesson in life—to take everything that happens to him as coming from the hand of GOD. That made him " content ", whatever his circumstances—poverty, or plenty ; up, or down ; " all things " came alike to him (12). Still, he did greatly appreciate all that these Philippian brethren had done for him (14), in his periods of physical distress. It was not only what it meant to him, in the satisfying of his need ; but, even more, what it meant to them, in the reward of kindness that will thereby accrue to them (17). He knew that the grace of generosity was great gain to the giver as well as to the getter—indeed, that " it is more blessed to give than to receive ". I wonder whether this saying of the Lord JESUS, unrecorded in the Gospels, was the theme of Paul's teaching " concerning giving and receiving " (15). If we are the Lord's, all we have is His, including our money—personal consecration is purse-and-all consecration ;

we are not just owners of it, but stewards of it; and " it is required in stewards that a man be found faithful ", I Corinthians iv. 2. Moreover, let it ever be remembered that we are to give " not grudgingly [though we don't want to], or of necessity [because we must] : for GOD loveth a cheerful [Gk., ? hilarious] giver ", II Corinthians ix. 7.

But how clearly this Epistle brings home to us the extent of *the Spiritual needs.* For it puts before us a picture of the Christian life at the highest level, filling our hearts with a great desire to come up to that standard, yet filling our minds with a great despair of ever reaching it. We know so well how far short we come, and how easily we fail ; and so we recognise our need of guidance and of grace to enable us to fulfil the purposes and plans that GOD has for us. Let us go back over the Epistle, and pick out at random some of His expectations of His children, in order that the sense of our need may become all the more definite, that it may turn us away from our inadequate selves, and that it may throw us all the more upon GOD. " *That your love may abound yet more and more* , i. 9—what a need is mirrored in that requirement : we need so much from Him, if this is to be fulfilled, " *Christ shall be magnified in my body* ", i. 20—if it be a fit body, or a frail body, it must needs be fortified, if its members are to be used in His happy service, endowed with physical strength, mental vigour, and spiritual power. " *Let your conversation be as it becometh the gospel of Christ* ", i. 27 —what need is evoked by this demand for a worthy demeanour and behaviour : complete consistency between creed and conduct, between lip and life, between profession and progression, is a vital necessity for a healthy Christian ; yet how great is his need if he is going to attain it. " *To suffer for His sake* ", i. 29 —Paul knew all about that ; and all that are called to it will need all the courage, all the endurance, to take it, whether it be suffering of body, even torture for their testimony ; or suffering of mind, for all the shame and obloquy heaped upon a Christian ; or suffering of heart, from the desertion of friends who have left them since they joined up with the Master. " *Let this mind be in you which was also in Christ Jesus* ", ii. 5—a mind of utter-most humility, sinking the seeming welfare of self for the weal of others ; thinking of those others as CHRIST once did, and always does ; we shall need a strong intincture of unearthly power if we are ever to achieve such a heavenly frame of mind. " *The sons of God without rebuke* ", ii. 15—how often we have to be rebuked by others ; yet here is a condition to which GOD'S children are summoned, a character in which GOD sees nothing, knows nothing, that calls for His serious, yet loving remonstrance ; how great their need if they are ever to attain this high stage of spiritual behaviour. " *This one thing I do* ", iii. 13—so many other voices are calling, so many other interests are clamant, that it is not always easy to give such undivided allegiance to the cause of CHRIST ; and, besides, the strength of temptation, and the weakness of self will combine to turn him from the path, if he cannot obtain what he needs to keep straight on. " *Rejoice in the Lord alway* ", iv. 4—we have just been considering it, and have reminded ourselves of all the forces of the world we live in that make such rejoicing difficult ; a man who stands face to face with such a demand knows full well how desperately he will need some great off-setting influence if he is to accede to it. " *Be careful for nothing* ", iv. 6—where is the man, or the woman, without anxiety ? The number of such non-worriers should be equivalent to the number of Christians. For them, but only for them, there is no need to worry ; but there is great need if they are not to. " *Those things . . . do* ", iv. 9—you'll need much if you are to heed such ; for Paul is offering himself to his Philippian friends as an example of Christian life for them to follow, as he, on his part, sought to follow CHRIST. Need, need, need—all the day, all the way. In the spiritual sense, the Christian is a bundle of needs ; still more so, if he is a bundle of nerves. From this stroll through the whole Epistle, stopping by the wayside to view some of the landmarks, let us retrace our footsteps back to the portion of the landscape, from which we wandered off. Here, then, we think of—

THE OPPORTUNITY OF SERVICE

" Ye lacked opportunity ", says verse 10. It is now something like ten years since the church at Philippi had the chance to do their friend service—they had the will, they had the wherewithal, but they hadn't the way. From verse 15 we get the impression that they had been among the prime contributors to the fund that Paul collected for the poor saints in Jerusalem, I Corinthians xvi. 1–5. But they had not forgotten his own needs either ; for, as he says, " ye sent once and again unto my necessity " (16). Then, from various circumstances, had come the long period wherein their gifts had perforce to cease. Now, however, " at the last your care of me hath flourished again " (10)—" budded forth again ", is Dean Alford's rendering. Epaphroditus had been able to bring from Philippi a whole lot of " things " (18) to relieve his destitution in the Roman prison.

Paul was deeply moved by this token of their abiding love and care for him. One recalls that incident in the life of the fugitive David when he was overheard to wish he could get a drink of water from the well of his native Bethlehem, and three of his men, at grave risk of their lives, ventured through the enemy lines, and brought back the water. David was completely overwhelmed by such devotion, and felt that he could not drink, but poured out the water, in sacrifice of thanksgiving before the Lord. Paul did not hesitate to partake of the victuals that his friends had sent ; but I imagine that his feelings were akin to David's. To the apostle, the gifts were " an odour of a sweet smell, a sacrifice acceptable, well-pleasing to GOD " (18).

The late Professor Deissmann, to whom the world is indebted for his discovery, through his archæological study of the unearthed papyri and ostraca of the Ancient East, that the New Testament is written, not in classical Greek, but in a vernacular, almost colloquial, form of Greek as used by the common people of the day, has an interesting suggestion concerning the phrase, " I have all " (18). He remarks that the word translated " have " was frequently used in a commercial sense, and was employed for describing the giving of a receipt. If his idea be adopted, the phrase would read, " I give a receipt in full ". In any case, that is the significance even of the Authorised Version, as it stands. It is Paul's acknowledgment that the Gift Parcel has arrived safely, and fully, to Paul's delight, and, we may say, verse 18, to GOD's delight.

Let it be taken to heart that these Philippians took their opportunity when it came. In the last case, they had waited for it all those years, on the look out for it ; and then, perhaps all of a sudden, the chance came, and they seized it with both hands. That is the New Testament advice. We have already quoted Galatians vi. 10, " As we have therefore opportunity, let us do good unto all men, especially unto them who are of the household of faith "—that is, our fellow-believers. And Hebrews xiii. 16 tells us, " to do good and to communicate [distribute] forget not, for with such sacrifices GOD is well pleased ". Opportunities for service often suddenly present themselves, and as suddenly pass : oh, to be quick to see and seize them. Unnoticed opportunities are like Browning's " angels ", that

> " . . . sit all day
> Beside you, and lie down at night by you,
> Who care not for their presence—muse—or sleep,
> And all at once they leave you—and you know them."

In the Christian sphere this is so often fraught with eternal significance. An opportunity of testimony presents itself— you are brought into touch with some person quite unarranged, and in your heart you feel the meeting is of GOD : say the intro- ductory word at once, ere the chance quickly is out of reach. What would have happened, I wonder, if Philip had lost the opportunity of hailing the Ethiopian chariot, that GOD had arranged to meet with the evangelist at that desert spot, Acts viii. 29. By some turn in the conversation among fellows, a chance occurs to put in a word for the Saviour—with love, with humility, and with tact grasp that chance. Eternal issues may hang on it. GOD does thus provide opportunities of service for His children, unless we habitually neglect them. I think it is not our respon- sibility to make them, but to take them. In trying to make opportunities, we so often only make blunders. If, at the opening of each day, we place ourselves at His disposal, He will so delightfully, as in Philip's case, make the Place, the Time, the Person to coincide—and will then give the Word to preach unto him JESUS. With what joy will you thus watch GOD working out His purposes through you. And so now, with evident appropriateness, we come to—

The Sufficiency of Power

" *I can do all things through* CHRIST *which strengtheneth me* " (13). There is no " do " in the Greek, so that from the broken sentence we almost get an impression of a man stirred, even excited, by the sudden realisation afresh that there is absolutely nothing required of him by GOD that he cannot do : he is complete master of every situation, he is equal to anything and everything. When things are glad, or sad ; when things are prosperous, or calamitous ; when things are gracious, or anxious—" I can ", says Paul ; I can stand up to life, whatever it brings, even if that means the imprisonment with all its deprivations and restrictions, and the daily, even hourly, irksomeness of the chain and soldier. He " can " ; and we can—for his secret is available to us. " Through [should be " in "] CHRIST which strengtheneth me ". It seems to me that, if " joy " is the characteristic of the Epistle, " in " is its secret—so often does it occur : and we haven't finished with it yet. In CHRIST, then, there is all the strength that I can possibly need—enough and to spare. Paul has the same thought in Romans viii. 37, " In all these things we are more than conquerors through Him that loved us "— conquerors (enough) ; more than (and to spare). But in what sense can we be more than conquerors ?   Surely, in not only overcoming, but in getting something out of what is overcome. Some trouble comes, and " through Him " we are enabled to bear it, and not to be bitter about it—that is to be a conqueror ; but out of our attitude towards the trouble there comes a deeper knowledge of GOD, and a new sympathy to help others " in the same boat "—that is something " more than " mere victory. What wonderful sufficiency is ours !

" *My God shall supply all your need according to His riches in glory by* [" *in* "] CHRIST JESUS " (19).   You have supplied all my need, he seems to say, now GOD will supply all your need.   And across the years he seems to say it to you and me also.   " *Your need* "—may be very big : so little to Him, but so large to you, therefore He will not belittle it, make light of it.   Yes, vast and varied may be our need.   " *My* GOD "—in all His majestic mightiness ;   Paul is allowed to reckon Him as " my " GOD : you and I are allowed the same privilege ;   up alongside of Him, our need does not seem so insuperably big, after all.   " *His riches* "—the other day, for a certain purpose, I had a cheque from a man drawn on his " No. 2 A/C ".   It would appear that GOD has at least four accounts—(1) " The riches of His goodness ", Romans ii. 4.   (2) " The riches of His wisdom ", Romans xi. 33. (3) " The riches of His grace ", Ephesians i. 7.   (4) " The riches of His glory ", Ephesians i. 18.   Out of one or other of His accounts there is abundance to meet all our need.   " *In glory* "—the Royal Bank of Heaven ;   and what a bank :   " where neither moth nor rust doth corrupt, and where thieves do not break through nor steal ", Matthew vi. 20.   " *According to* "—not just " out of ", as the verse is so often misquoted.   A millionaire might give a tramp a shilling " out of " his riches ;   but how greater would be a help " according to ", that is, after the measure of His riches—the first, a parsimonious gift ;   the other, a princely gift.   This latter is the Divine manner.

So closes the passage, on the note, not of any praise to us, for anything we may be, or may have done, but of acknowledgment that it is all of Him.   The " glory ", then, is His, and shall be His " for ever and ever " !

XVI

GOOD-BYE, SAINTS !

PHILIPPIANS iv. 21–23

We come now to the closing salutations of this delightful Letter. " The salutation of me Paul with mine own hand ", I Corinthians xvi. 21. " Ye see how large a letter [perhaps, with what large letters] I have written unto you with mine own hand ", Galatians vi. 11. " The salutation by the hand of me Paul ", Colossians iv. 18—" remember my bonds ", he adds, possibly by way of explanation of his large, bad writing : you can't write very well when your wrist is in chains. " The salutation of Paul with mine own hand, which is the token in every epistle : so I write ", II Thessalonians iii. 17. It would appear that it was his practice, after dictating his letters to an amanuensis, to take the stylo, and, in his own handwriting, to add a concluding word of farewell salutation. Doubtless to the great delight of his readers. I feel pretty sure that these closing three verses belong to the same category ; and that when Epaphroditus delivers the letter, all those Philippian Christians will gather round to hear the thrice-welcome communication, and that when he shows them the actual manuscript, they will recognise with glee the authentic caligraphy. Dear old Paul, his writing is as bad as ever—but what else can you expect : " Remember, my bonds " ! So he addresses himself to " the saints ". I do not propose to deal here now with Who, and What they are—we went into that in our first chapter—but Where they are. We consider, therefore, the suggestions of their four locations.

Saints—in the Place of Blessing

" *Salute every saint in* Christ Jesus " (21). Here is the last occurrence of this wonderful " in "—as we have seen over and over again in the course of the Epistle, all that we are, all that we do, all that we can, all that we have, is " in " Him—as old John Newton sang,

> " My never failing treasury, filled
> With boundless stores of grace."

This is our dwelling-place, our fount of blessing. Do you notice that it says, not " all ", which would indicate the company of believers as a whole, but " every ", which represents that company as individuals. Christians are not saved in the mass but as separate persons. The old word may be applied, " Ye shall be gathered one by one ", Isaiah xxvii. 12. And we have abundant evidence in the Gospels that, while " I have compassion on the multitude ", Matthew xv. 32, He gave Himself un-reservedly, untiringly, to the blessing of individuals—what an amount of time He gave to the ones : as Nicodemus, and the Samaritan woman ; how wonderfully He prayed for the particular person : as in Luke xxii. 31-2—" Simon, Simon, behold, Satan hath desired to have you [all], that he may sift you as wheat, but I have prayed for thee [personally] that thy faith fail not ". And how conscious of the individual He was even in the crowd —" His disciples said unto Him, Thou seest the multitude thronging Thee, and sayest Thou, who touched Me ? " Mark v. 31. He was aware of that one in the crowd and of her need. Yes, Paul, we note the distinction between your " all ", and your " every ". Each one of the everyone has one thing in common. They are amazingly different in so many ways—some have made very little progress in the Christian life ; some are at a complete standstill ; some have come into a very high level of spiritual experience ; but satisfactory or unsatisfactory, each alike has this enormous privilege and blessing, that he is " in CHRIST JESUS "—so that the satisfactory may grow yet further, and the unsatisfactory may become what He wants him to be. Praise GOD for such a place of blessing. What an inspiration it might be if our waking thought each morning were, to repeat, " In CHRIST JESUS ".

SAINTS—IN THE PLACE OF PRIVILEGE

" *The brethren which are with me* " (21). " The companions who visited him most frequently in his imprisonment," says Plummer. Probably Tychicus, of the Ephesians, Timothy and Epaphroditus, of the Philippians ; possibly, Onesimus, who, erstwhile thief that he had been, was now amongst the blessed body of " brethren " ; Aristarchus, " my fellow-prisoner ", Mark, Jesus Justus, Epaphras, and Dr. Luke, of the Colossians. All these were with the apostle in Rome, and were apparently allowed to go and see him in his prison room, and to go on errands for him. But, what a privilege to be with him like that—to help him with his correspondence, to listen to his talk of the things of

GOD, to join with him in his prayers, to watch his patience and cheerfulness that could enable him to write such a letter as the Joy Way. Again we say, what a privilege !

How great and deep can be the influence upon us lesser men by our association with the big men of the Kingdom of GOD. H. M. Stanley bore glad testimony to the spiritual influence that the godly life of Dr. Livingstone had on him during the time he stayed with him, after he had " found " him, in Darkest Africa. How can I measure the effect of my working under Dr. R. A. Torrey, during his month's wonderful Mission at the Royal Albert Hall, London ; or thank GOD enough for the influence on my life and ministry these many years, of my beloved friend, that great man of GOD, Richard Hudson Pope, to whom I owe more than I can ever say, or pay; or to that remarkable man, Robert Charles Joynt, my boyhood's vicar, at Christ Church, Gipsy Hill. To what a host of men and women I am indebted ! You, too, my reader, can bear like witness to those who have meant much to you—first leading you to CHRIST, and then leading you on for CHRIST. Can we, I wonder, such small people, be enabled to exercise any little degree of such influence on any life ? Someone, perhaps, coming up behind. At any rate, let us, on the negative side, be careful not to exercise a bad, or doubtful, influence—as we quoted earlier, " Make straight paths for your feet lest that which is lame be turned out of the way," Hebrews xii. 13.

SAINTS—IN THE PLACE OF COMMUNITY

" *All the saints salute you* " (22). He has thought of them as individuals, now it is the company as a united body. They all, as a church, in Rome, send their love to them all, the church in Philippi. It is a fact of very great importance, both for the spiritual welfare of the Christian, as also for the strength of the testimony to the world, that each soul won to CHRIST should remember that he is thus " born again " into a family, into a company, and that no believer can be properly developed, in the things of GOD, unless he realises, and exercises, the church life, unless he have this sense, and obligation, of community. The Christian songster is not just a soloist, but a member of a choir ; the Christian soldier is not just a solitary figure, but a member of an army ; the Christian scholar is not just a privately tutored learner, but a member of a school ; the Christian son is not just a lonely child, but a member of a family ; the Christian sprinter is not just an individual performer, but a member of a

team. " For by one SPIRIT are we all baptised into one body,"
I Corinthians xii. 13.

So let us be zealous in the discharge of our responsibilities in
connection with whatever outward body of believers we happen
to belong—pulling our weight in all its life and activity. We
shall, of course, fail in that if we are for ever running after dis-
tinguished preachers in other churches, or rushing off to exciting
campaigns far and wide and never settling to the ordinary life of
work and worship in our own church. We can't grow strong
in the spiritual life if we are continually feeding upon the attractive
and delightful pastries of special missions and movements, we
need normally the steady, solid feeding upon the bread and meat
of the Word.

Moreover, let us see to it that our relationship with our fellow-
members of the Christian community is all that it ought to be as
members of the same Family of GOD. It is sad beyond measure
that we sometimes find in churches such an unholy brood of
grudges, cliques, criticisms, even antagonisms. The Philippian
church was not free of such unworthy squabbles, as we have seen.
Anyhow, my reader, be sure that *you* are not party to any of
these unchristian things. Differences of opinion, of course,
there must be, but why cannot they be held, and stated, in love ?
How grievous it is to find church members at " logger-heads ".
Let us heed the injunction, in this as in all matters, " Grieve not
the HOLY SPIRIT of GOD, whereby ye are sealed unto the day of
redemption," Ephesians iv. 30. " endeavouring to keep the unity
of the SPIRIT in the bond of peace," verse 3.

SAINTS—IN THE PLACE OF SURPRISE

" *They that are of Cæsar's household* " (22). Lightfoot has
established the fact that " Cæsar's household " was a description
embracing the whole wide range of imperial employees—not
just his family and house servants, but his slaves, his army,
his officials ; the most important and the most insignificant,
both near and far. It would be amongst these that the prevailing
idolatry would be likely to be more rampant, especially the
fairly recently fostered cult of the worship of the emperor. Yet,
we get the surprising news that there had arisen " saints in
Cæsar's household " !

It is not difficult to realise how this came about. Take such a
phrase as we saw in i. 13, " My bonds in CHRIST are manifest
in all the palace ". There is more in that than appears on the
surface—this prisoner was attracting some very special attention,

everybody was talking about him, they had never had one like him. Those soldiers who were placed on the rota for guarding him were, at least some of them, not only interested, but intrigued and impressed. There were some whom this prisoner led to the Saviour ; and on their next term of duty with him there would be Christian fellowship and instruction. One such, perhaps, would be thrilled as Paul made up a sermon on the pieces of his armour, and dictated it as part of a letter he was writing : Ephesians vi. 14–18. And now the apostle includes the little band of military converts—the first Soldiers' Christian Association—in the greetings to the Philippian believers. It was a lovely surprise to find that happy company in such a place.

It only goes to show—doesn't it—that you can bear your witness, and see fruit, in the most unlikely places. Paul was not going to be silenced because he was in prison—he would find opportunity for Christian testimony, wherever he was, and whatever his circumstances. Wasn't it when he was ill at Troas, that he won the doctor, Dr. Luke, to CHRIST ? We don't know that ; but it was so like the apostle : always at it. And the results came. Are you in a situation seemingly uncongenial to Christian witness—an office, a factory, a shop, a club, a home, a circle. Be on the look-out—and, perhaps all of a sudden, most unexpectedly, you may get a chance to say a word for the Master to some individual, which by the work of the HOLY SPIRIT shall lead to conversion. There is no place where the SPIRIT'S influence is impossible, though many where it might be surprising. Let us seek only that we may walk closely with GOD, so that, at any moment, He may be able to arrange the opportunity for us to help some soul heavenward.

> " Lord, lay some soul upon my heart,
>   And bless that soul through me ;
>   And may I humbly do my part
>   To bring that soul to Thee."

Be that our attitude, and our prayer, wherever we may be called to be—however unlikely it may all seem to be.

. . . .

" *The grace of our Lord* JESUS CHRIST *be with you all. Amen.*" Almost the first word of the Epistle was " grace " (i. 2) ; and now, almost the last word is " grace " (iv. 23). Type of the Christian life itself—which begins in grace, Ephesians ii. 8 ; which is pursued all along in grace, I Corinthians xv. 10 ; and which will usher us into eternal bliss by that same grace.

> " Oh, to grace how great a debtor
> Daily I'm constrained to be."

What better, prayerful, good wish could the apostle close his letter with. All kinds of saints, and the whole body of saints —" every ", and " all "—find the variety of their need met, and the sufficiency of their problems met, in this all-embracing and eternal grace of GOD. And the " great grace " of Acts iv. 33 will soon be followed by the " great joy " of Acts viii. 8—this is the Joy Way. Amen !

THE EPISTLE OF PAUL THE APOSTLE TO THE
PHILIPPIANS

CHAPTER 1.

PAUL and Timotheus, the servants of Jesus Christ, to all the saints in Christ Jesus which are at Philippi, with the bishops and deacons :

2 Grace be unto you, and peace, from God our Father, and from the Lord Jesus Christ.

3 I thank my God upon every remembrance of you.

4 Always in every prayer of mine for you all making request with joy.

5 For your fellowship in the gospel from the first day until now ;

6 Being confident of this very thing, that he which hath begun a good work in you will perform it until the day of Jesus Christ :

7 Even as it is meet for me to think this of you all, because I have you in my heart ; inasmuch as both in my bonds, and in the defence and confirmation of the gospel, ye are all partakers of my grace.

8 For God is my record, how greatly I long after you all in the bowels of Jesus Christ.

9 And this I pray, that your love may abound yet more and more in knowledge and in all judgment ;

10 That ye may approve things that are excellent ; that ye may be sincere and without offence till the day of Christ ;

11 Being filled with the fruits of righteousness, which are by Jesus Christ, unto the glory and praise of God.

12 But I would ye should understand, brethren, that the things which happened unto me have fallen out rather unto the furtherance of the gospel ;

13 So that my bonds in Christ are manifest in all the palace, and in all other places ;

14 And many of the brethren in the Lord, waxing confident by my bonds, are much more bold to speak the word without fear

15 Some indeed preach Christ even of envy and strife ; and some also of good will :

16 The one preach Christ of contention, not sincerely, supposing to add affliction to my bonds :

17 But the other of love, knowing that I am set for the defence of the gospel.

18 What then ? notwithstanding, every way, whether in pretence, or in truth, Christ is preached ; and I therein do rejoice, yea, and will rejoice.

19 For I know that this shall turn to my salvation through your prayer, and the supply of the Spirit of Jesus Christ,

20 According to my earnest expectation and my hope, that in nothing I shall be ashamed, but that with all boldness, as always, so now also Christ shall be magnified in my body, whether it be by life, or by death.

21 For to me to live is Christ, and to die is gain.

22 But if I live in the flesh, this is the fruit of my labour : yet what I shall choose I wot not.

23 For I am in a strait betwixt two, having a desire to depart, and to be with Christ ; which is far better :

24 Nevertheless to abide in the flesh is more needful for you.

25 And having this confidence, I know that I shall abide and continue with you all for your furtherance and joy of faith ;

26 That your rejoicing may be more abundant in Jesus Christ for me by my coming to you again.

27 Only let your conversation be as it becometh the gospel of Christ : that whether I come and see you, or else be absent, I may hear of your affairs, that ye stand fast in one spirit, with one mind striving together for the faith of the gospel ;

28 And in nothing terrified by your adversaries : which is to them an evident token of perdition, but to you of salvation, and that of God.

29 For unto you it is given in the behalf of Christ, not only to believe on him, but also to suffer for his sake ;

30 Having the same conflict which ye saw in me, and now hear *to be* in me.

CHAPTER 2.

IF *there be* therefore any consolation in Christ, if any comfort of love, if any fellowship of the Spirit, if any bowels and mercies.

2 Fulfil ye my joy, that ye be likeminded, having the same love, *being* of one accord, of one mind.

3 *Let* nothing *be done* through strife or vainglory; but in lowliness of mind let each esteem other better than themselves.

4 Look not every man on his own things, but every man also on the things of others.

5 Let this mind be in you, which was also in Christ Jesus:

6 Who, being in the form of God, thought it not robbery to be equal with God :

7 But made himself of no reputation, and took upon him the form of a servant, and was made in the likeness of men :

8 And being found in fashion as a man, he humbled himself, and became obedient unto death, even the death of the cross.

9 Wherefore God also hath highly exalted him, and given him a name which is above every name :

10 That at the name of Jesus every knee should bow, of *things* in heaven, and *things* in earth, and *things* under the earth ;

11 And *that* every tongue should confess that Jesus Christ *is* Lord, to the glory of God the Father.

12 Wherefore, my beloved, as ye have always obeyed, not as in my presence only, but now much more in my absence, work out your own salvation with fear and trembling.

13 For it is God which worketh in you both to will and to do of *his* good pleasure.

14 Do all things without murmurings and disputings ;

15 That ye may be blameless and harmless, the sons of God, without rebuke, in the midst of a crooked and perverse nation, among whom ye shine as lights in the world ;

16 Holding forth the word of life ; that I may rejoice in the day of Christ, that I have not run in vain, neither laboured in vain.

17 Yea, and if I be offered upon the sacrifice and service of your faith, I joy, and rejoice with you all.

18 For the same cause also do ye joy, and rejoice with me.

19 But I trust in the Lord Jesus to send Timotheus shortly unto you, that I also may be of good comfort, when I know your state.

20 For I have no man likeminded, who will naturally care for your state.

21 For all seek their own, not the things which are Jesus Christ's.

22 But ye know the proof of him, that, as a son with the father, he hath served with me in the gospel.

23 Him therefore I hope to send presently, so soon as I shall see how it will go with me.

24 But I trust in the Lord that I also myself shall come shortly.

25 Yet I supposed it necessary to send to you Epaphroditus, my brother, and companion in labour, and fellowsoldier, but your messenger, and he that ministered to my wants.

26 For he longed after you all, and was full of heaviness, because that ye had heard that he had been sick.

27 For indeed he was sick nigh unto death : but God had mercy on him ; and not on him only, but on me also, lest I should have sorrow upon sorrow.

28 I sent him therefore the more carefully, that, when ye see him again, ye may rejoice, and that I may be the less sorrowful.

29 Receive him therefore in the Lord with all gladness ; and hold such in reputation :

30 Because for the work of Christ he was nigh unto death, not regarding his life, to supply your lack of service toward me.

CHAPTER 3.

FINALLY, my brethren, rejoice in the Lord. To write the same things to you, to me indeed *is* not grievous, but for you *it is* safe.

2 Beware of dogs, beware of evil workers, beware of the concision.

3 For we are the circumcision, which worship God in the spirit, and rejoice in Christ Jesus, and have no confidence in the flesh.

4 Though I might also have confidence in the flesh. If any other man thinketh that he hath whereof he might trust in the flesh, I more :

5 Circumcised the eighth day, of the stock of Israel, *of* the tribe of Benjamin, an Hebrew of the Hebrews ; as touching the law, a Pharisee ;

6 Concerning zeal, persecuting the church ; touching the righteousness which is in the law, blameless.

7 But what things were gain to me, those I counted loss for Christ.

8 Yea doubtless, and I count all things *but* loss for the excellency of the knowledge of Christ Jesus my Lord : for whom I have suffered the loss of all things, and do count them *but* dung, that I may win Christ.

9 And he found in him, not having mine own righeousness, which is of the law, but that which is through the faith of Christ, the righteousness which is of God by faith :

10 That I may know him, and the power of his resurrection, and the fellowship of his sufferings, being made conformable unto his death ;

11 If by any means I might attain unto the resurrection of the dead.

12 Not as though I had already attained, either were already perfect : but I follow after, if that I may apprehend that for which also I am apprehended of Christ Jesus.

13 Brethren, I count not myself to have apprehended : but *this* one thing *I do*, forgetting those things which are behind, and reaching forth unto those things which are before,

14 I press toward the mark for the prize of the high calling of God in Christ Jesus.

15 Let us therefore, as many as be perfect, be thus minded : and if in any thing ye be otherwise minded, God shall reveal even this unto you.

16 Nevertheless, whereto we have already attained, let us walk by the same rule, let us mind the same thing.

17 Brethren, be followers together of me, and mark them which walk so as ye have us for an ensample.

18 (For many walk, of whom I have told you often, and now tell you even weeping, *that they are* the enemies of the cross of Christ :

19 Whose end *is* destruction, whose God *is their* belly, and *whose* glory *is* in their shame, who mind earthly things.)

20 For our conversation is in heaven ; from whence also we look for the Saviour, the Lord Jesus Christ :

21 Who shall change our vile body, that it may be fashioned like unto his glorious body, according to the working whereby he is able even to subdue all things unto himself.

CHAPTER 4.

THEREFORE, my brethren dearly beloved and longed for, my joy and crown, so stand fast in the Lord, *my* dearly beloved.

2 I beseech Euodias, and beseech Syntyche, that they be of the same mind in the Lord.

3 And I intreat thee also, true yokefellow, help those women which laboured with me in the gospel, with Clement also, and *with* other my fellowlabourers, whose names *are* in the book of life.

4 Rejoice in the Lord alway *and* again I say, Rejoice.

5 Let your moderation be known unto all men. The Lord *is* at hand.

6 Be careful for nothing ; but in every thing by prayer and supplication with thanksgiving let your requests be made known unto God.

7 And the peace of God, which passeth all understanding, shall keep your hearts and minds through Christ Jesus.

8 Finally, brethren, whatsoever things are true, whatsoever things *are* honest, whatsoever things *are* just, whatsoever things *are* pure, whatsoever things *are* lovely, whatsoever things *are* of good report ; if *there be* any virtue, and if *there be* any praise, think on these things.

9 Those things, which ye have both learned, and received, and heard, and seen in me, do : and the God of peace shall be with you.

10 But I rejoiced in the Lord greatly, that now at the last your care of me hath flourished again ; wherein ye were also careful, but ye lacked opportunity.

11 Not that I speak in respect of want : for I have learned, in whatsoever state I am, *therewith* to be content.

12 I know both how to be abased, and I know how to abound ; every where and in all things I am instructed both to be full and to be hungry, both to abound and to suffer need.

13 I can do all things through Christ which strengtheneth me.

14 Notwithstanding ye have well done, that ye did communicate with my affliction.

15 Now ye Philippians know also, that in the beginning of the gospel, when I departed from Macedonia, no church communicated with me as concerning giving and receiving, but ye only.

16 For even in Thessalonica ye sent once and again unto my necessity.

17 Not because I desire a gift : but I desire fruit that may abound to your account.

18 But I have all, and abound : I am full, having received of Epaphroditus the things *which were sent* from you, an odour of a sweet smell, a sacrifice acceptable, wellpleasing to God.

19 But my God shall supply all your need according to his riches in glory by Christ Jesus.

20 Now unto God and our Father *be* glory for ever and ever. Amen.

21 Salute every saint in Christ Jesus. The brethren which are with me greet you.

22 All the saints salute you, chiefly they that are of Cæsar's household.

23 The grace of our Lord Jesus Christ *be* with you all. Amen.